Language Arts Learning Centers

for the

Primary Grades

Carol A. Poppe
Nancy A. Van Matre

illustrated by Nancy A. Van Matre

JOSSEY-BASS
A Wiley Imprint
www.josseybass.com

Copyright © 1991 by John Wiley & Sons, Inc. All rights reserved.

Published by Jossey-Bass
A Wiley Imprint
989 Market Street, San Francisco, CA 94103-1741   www.josseybass.com

No part of this publication may be reproduced, stored in a retrieval system, or transmitted in any form
or by any means, electronic, mechanical, photocopying, recording, scanning, or otherwise, except as
permitted under Section 107 or 108 of the 1976 United States Copyright Act, without either the prior
written permission of the Publisher, or authorization through payment of the appropriate per-copy
fee to the Copyright Clearance Center, Inc., 222 Rosewood Drive, Danvers, MA 01923, (978) 750-8400,
fax (978) 646-8600, or on the web at www.copyright.com. Requests to the Publisher for permission
should be addressed to the Permissions Department, John Wiley & Sons, Inc., 111 River Street,
Hoboken, NJ 07030, (201) 748-6011, fax (201) 748-6008, e-mail: permcoordinator@wiley.com.

Permission is given for individual classroom teachers to reproduce the pages and illustrations for
classroom use. Reproduction of these materials for an entire school system is strictly forbidden.

Jossey-Bass books and products are available through most bookstores. To contact Jossey-Bass directly
call our Customer Care Department within the U.S. at (800) 956-7739, outside the U.S. at (317) 572-
3986 or fax (317) 572-4002.

Jossey-Bass also publishes its books in a variety of electronic formats. Some content that appears in
print may not be available in electronic books.

A special thank you to my students in my Clinton Elementary first grade class of
1989—1990 who helped with some of the very special illustrations in this book.
                                                                —"Mrs. Miller"

Library of Congress Cataloging-in-Publication Data
Poppe, Carol A.
    Language arts learning centers for the primary grades / Carol A.
Poppe and Nancy A. Van Matre ; illustrated by Nancy A. Van Matre.
        p. cm.
    ISBN 0–87628–505–1
    1. Language arts (Primary) 2. Classroom learning centers.
3. Education, Primary—Activity programs. I. Van Matre, Nancy A.
II. Title
LB1528.P67   1991
372.6—dc20   90-47992

FIRST EDITION
PB Printing 10 9 8 7 6 5 4 3 2

About the Authors

CAROL A. POPPE received her B.A. degree from Ohio University and has taken several graduate courses at Oakland University and Siena Heights College. Mrs. Poppe has 25 years of teaching experience at the first- and second-grade levels. She and her husband, Michael, enjoy camping and have traveled to most of the states and Canadian provinces. She has three daughters, Nancy, Molly, and Jenny, who live in Michigan, Ohio, and Tennessee, respectively.

NANCY A. VAN MATRE, who received her B.A. degree and M.A. degree in Reading from Eastern Michigan University, has been actively teaching grades 1 through 3 since 1975. She resides in Ann Arbor with her husband, Bruce Miller, and their two sons, Nick and Jason.

During the past fifteen years, the authors have used their learning centers as an integral part of their classroom schedules at Clinton (Michigan) Community School. After presenting workshops, they realized that other educators wanted to begin a learning center system, but needed management techniques, learning center activity ideas, and shortcuts.

In an effort to help other educators, the authors have also written *Science Learning Centers for the Primary Grades* (1985), *K–3 Science Activities Kit* (1988), and *Social Studies Learning Centers for the Primary Grades* (1989), each published by The Center for Applied Research in Education.

About This Book

Language Arts Learning Centers for the Primary Grades will help you effectively develop and manage a language arts learning center system in your classroom. Four language arts learning center units are provided, with over one hundred activities using children's literature as a catalyst:

Dr. Seuss and His Friends

Bears

Dogs

American Tall Tales and Legends

The language arts units are designed to promote the growth of communication abilities—listening, speaking, reading, writing, and thinking—of every student. Easy-to-use, reproducible, time-saving file folder directions are included for the four units.

The skills taught and reinforced in each learning center unit include those listed on the skills chart shown below.

Skills

Language Arts Units	Reading	Listening	Speaking	Summarizing	Using Reference Materials	Creative Writing	Fine-Motor Coordination	Spelling	Creating/Art	Math	Science/Health	Computer	Teacher's Choice/Open-Ended
DR. SEUSS AND HIS FRIENDS													
Learning Centers	x	x	x		x	x	x	x	x	x	x	x	x
Enrichment Activities	x	x	x	x	x	x	x	x	x				
BEARS													
Learning Centers	x	x	x		x	x	x		x	x	x	x	x
Enrichment Activities	x	x	x	x	x	x	x	x			x		
DOGS													
Learning Centers	x	x	x		x	x	x		x	x	x	x	x
Enrichment Activities	x	x	x	x	x	x	x	x	x				
AMERICAN TALL TALES AND LEGENDS													
Learning Centers	x	x	x		x	x	x		x	x	x	x	x
Enrichment Activities	x		x	x	x	x	x	x	x				

Each learning center activity is based on a famous children's book relating to these themes. The activities may be used at learning centers as outlined in the management part of this book or they may be taken individually to be used with the entire group. Numerous ideas are suggested for adapting the activities to a multilevel or multiage classroom. The activities were designed for grades K–3 and are appropriate for accelerated and special needs students.

Each of the four units contains:

1. Eight language arts learning center theme activities from the content areas of communication, math, art, science, motor, and computer.
2. Reproducible illustrated direction pages designed for mounting on file folders. The teacher's directions for each learning center include:
   a. Skills taught
   b. Materials needed
   c. Materials preparation
   d. Bibliography of books to be used
   e. Detailed directions for the file folder activities
3. Reproducible full-page activity pages to use at the learning centers.
4. An illustrated bulletin board activity.
5. Parent letters that explain the learning center activities.
6. Parent feedback letters encouraging parent-to-teacher communication.
7. A group activity that can be done by the entire class.
8. A reproducible learning center marker.
9. A center list of the eight learning centers to be used as a reference in a lesson plan book and in the materials storage box.
10. An open-ended learning center to allow you to choose any appropriate grade-level skill you wish to emphasize, then adapt it for the center (such as reviewing decoding skills or reinforcing an appropriate math skill).
11. "Takeoff" suggestions for each center as springboards to extended activities.
12. A learning center activity designed for use with a classroom computer.

In addition, each unit contains enrichment activities, including a whole-group activity. Practical teacher suggestions are given for using reproducible enrichment activity pages for spelling practice, creative writing, read-at-home ideas and awards, book report or research activities, and unit summaries.

A bibliography of all the books mentioned in each chapter follows the learning center sections. This bibliography will assist you in locating the books you will need for the centers and enrichment activities.

A special feature of *Language Arts Learning Centers for the Primary Grades* is the section called Enjoying Language Arts. It details a variety of motivating ideas to encourage your students to share their experiences in literature within the school, with family, and with community. You will also find practical ideas for organizing parents to assist you in the preparation of the many materials necessary for a stimulating language arts program.

By enthusiastically sharing books and authors with your children, you will encourage them to discover the joy of reading. As they complete the learning center activities, you will also find that the children increase their ability to work independently and more creatively.

Carol A. Poppe
Nancy A. Van Matre

Dedicated to Michael, Bruce, Nick, and Jason for their love and patience.

For Michael and Jason, who faithfully weathered the storms of their fourth book voyage.

For Bruce and Nick, who were initiated on their maiden voyage.

Maybe a smooth "cruise" ship next time, fellows?

To the Teacher

The activities in the language arts units accompany familiar books that you will need to obtain from a library or a bookstore. You may use the bibliography that follows the learning center sections to assist you in locating the books.

HOW TO INTRODUCE THE LANGUAGE ARTS LEARNING CENTER BOOKS

The language arts units are designed to be used at learning centers. The students will need to read or listen to the book featured at each learning center prior to beginning the learning center activity.

The way you choose to introduce the books will vary, depending on your students' ages. Some ideas are

1. The student reads the book independently at the learning center.
2. You may read the books aloud to the whole class prior to beginning a language arts unit.
3. You may prepare a cassette tape of the book for student use with a tape recorder at the learning center.
4. You or the students may use audiovisual materials such as filmstrips, films, video cassettes, and so on.
5. Guest readers may be invited to your room to read the book. These may include parents, other staff members, administrators, grandparents, assistants, or older students.

The reproducible Student Activity Pages go with each story. You may photocopy the reproducible pages in this book or make spirit masters or thermal copies from a photocopy.

Each language arts unit contains one center activity listed as "teacher's choice." It is an open-ended activity designed to review a math or phonics skill specific to the students' grade level. You will need to determine the skill you wish to review prior to duplicating most teacher's choice activities.

Additional ways that you can use the books with your class as a whole or small group are suggested in the Takeoff and Enrichment Activities sections of each unit.

CONSTRUCTING THE LANGUAGE ARTS DIRECTION FILE FOLDERS

The directions for each of the language arts learning centers in this book are designed to fit on 12″ × 18″ file folders. Brightly colored file folders are attractive for this purpose. A glue stick works well for mounting the direction pages. Crayons or water-base marking pens may be used to color the illustrations and numbers. (Prior to mounting any directions, be sure the other side of the page has been duplicated for future use.) Once constructed, the direction file folders may become part of a permanent collection of language arts units.

How to Make the Direction File Folder

1. Glue the Teacher Directions to the back of the file folder. (This visual aid is helpful to you in organizing the necessary materials for the learning center.)

2. Glue the Directions for File Folder Activities to the adjacent back side of the file folder.

3. Color the pictures on the student File Folder Directions Page.

4. Color the numbers orange on the student File Folder Directions Page. (Use the same format for all the file folders.)

5. Glue the student File Folder Directions Page to the front of the file folder.

6. Laminate or use clear self-stick vinyl to cover all the direction file folders.

Optional Ideas for Making Direction File Folders

1. Additional theme pictures from magazines, catalogs, and so on, may be glued to the front side of the file folder (adjacent to the student File Folder Directions Page).

2. A 10″ × 13″ envelope with a Student Activity Page mounted on it may be attached to the front side of the file folder (adjacent to the student File Folder Directions Page). The envelope is used as a container for the Student Activity Page.

A Direction File Folder Tip for the Nonreader or Beginning Reader

Make a set of corresponding File Folder Directions numbers on 1″ squares of orange construction paper with a black marking pen. Staple or tape these numbers to the Student Activity Page container, books, tape recorder, games, and so on, at the learning center. The numbers assist the student with less developed reading skills to complete the activities in sequential order.

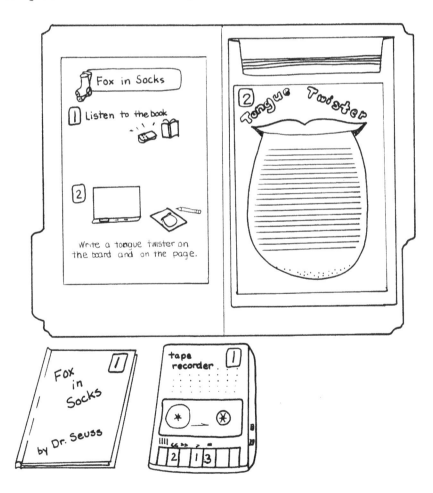

USING THE COMPUTER FOR LANGUAGE ARTS LEARNING CENTER ACTIVITIES:

There are activities in each Language Arts unit that are designed to be used with a computer. (If a computer is unavailable, alternative options are suggested.) The extent to which you use a computer will depend on the kind of computer, types of software available, and the computer's accessibility.

Scheduling the Computer

1. Ideally, the computer should be set up at a learning center (near an electrical outlet) for an eight-day period. The child uses the computer at his or her regularly scheduled learning center time.
2. The child could be sent to use the computer in your school's media center or computer lab during his or her learning center time.
   a. Advanced planning is required with a school support person (media specialist, parent aide, or older student aide) to schedule and direct the student.
   b. Rules for leaving the classroom and using the computer should be established with the children.

Advantages of Using a Computer

1. Each child has an opportunity to use the computer for approximately thirty minutes during an eight-day period, eliminating teacher scheduling of turns.
2. A variety of computer skills can be presented and reinforced such as keyboarding, word processing, graphic design, and printer usage.
3. Children enjoy using it and catch on very rapidly to the directions.
4. It becomes a manipulative learning center instead of a pencil and paper activity.
5. It requires a minimum amount of record keeping.

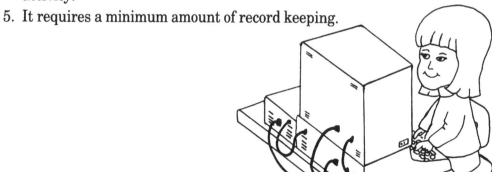

How to Prepare Language Arts Learning Center Materials:

You may wish to involve students or parents in the preparation of materials for the learning center activities. You will need to refer to the "Materials needed" and "Materials preparation" sections of the "Teacher's Directions" to plan the tasks.

A few days prior to beginning a new Language Arts unit, divide the students into small groups. Assign each group various jobs such as designing bulletin boards, coloring direction file folders, making patterns, cutting materials, and preparing cassette tapes. You may want to have a few parents assisting the students. You may prefer to have parents work independently preparing the materials depending on the age group of your students.

Storing the Language Arts Units:

Once constructed, the Direction for File Folders learning center activities may become part of a permanent collection of Language Arts units. It is helpful to keep the direction file folders and materials for each Language Arts unit in a large plastic container (18 gallon size) with a lid or a large cardboard storage box approximately 29 by 16 by 12 inches high with a lid. The same size boxes can be easily labeled, carried, and stacked utilizing a minimum amount of floor space. A copy of the Language Arts Learning Centers List may be taped inside the lid for easy reference.

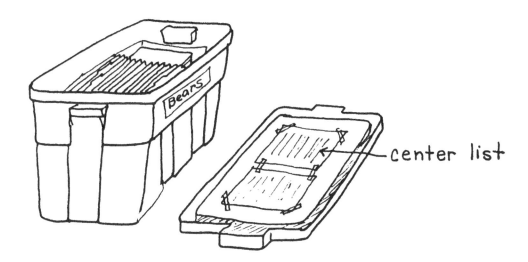

Contents

Management

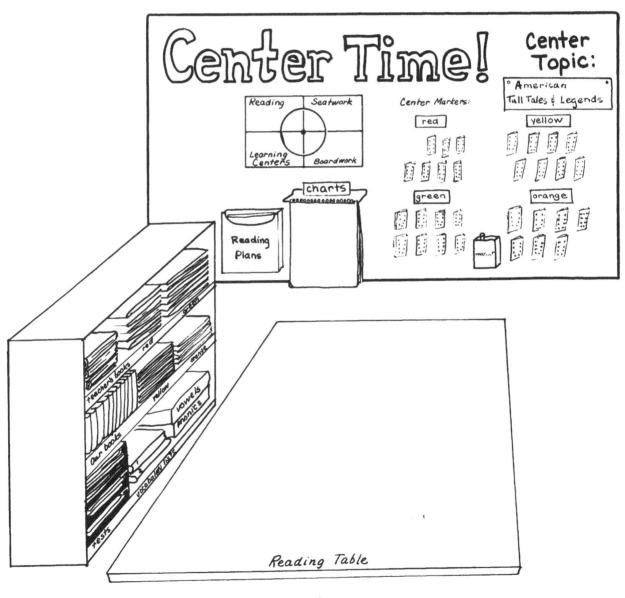

The language arts units in this book are designed for use at learning centers. The learning center management techniques described here have been used in our classrooms since 1976. By experimenting, we have changed and refined many of our learning center ideas. Educators who have attended our learning center workshop presentations have also given us valuable feedback.

A brief synopsis of this system is given in this chapter. More specific details are described extensively in the books *Science Learning Centers for the Primary Grades* by Carol A. Poppe and Nancy A. Van Matre (West Nyack, NY: The Center for Applied Research in Education, 1985) and *Social Studies Learning Centers for the Primary Grades* by Carol A. Poppe and Nancy A. Van Matre (West Nyack, NY: The Center for Applied Research in Education, 1989).

Additional learning center ideas are given in *K–3 Science Activities Kit* by Carol A. Poppe and Nancy A. Van Matre (West Nyack, NY: The Center for Applied Research in Education, 1988).

HOW TO MANAGE A LEARNING CENTER SYSTEM

This system features learning center unit activities as an integral part of the daily schedule.

The children are taught in a traditional manner for the initial three weeks of the school year. All the children are assigned morning seatwork. The teacher works with small groups of children to assess their reading ability.

The teacher then establishes four reading groups based on ability. Each group is given a color name: red, yellow, orange, and green.

After the four groups are established, the children are introduced to a new morning routine (see the Morning Schedule on page 3). The children move every half hour to four areas of the classroom to do seatwork, boardwork, reading, and learning center activities (one child per learning center).

A color wheel displayed near the reading area aids in the clockwise movement of the four groups to the four areas of the room.

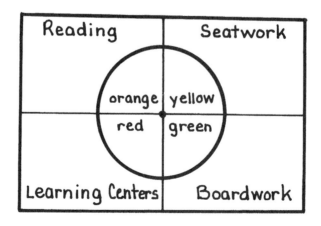

Morning Schedule

8:30 to 9:00   Whole class is at seatwork and boardwork desks for opening and morning work directions.

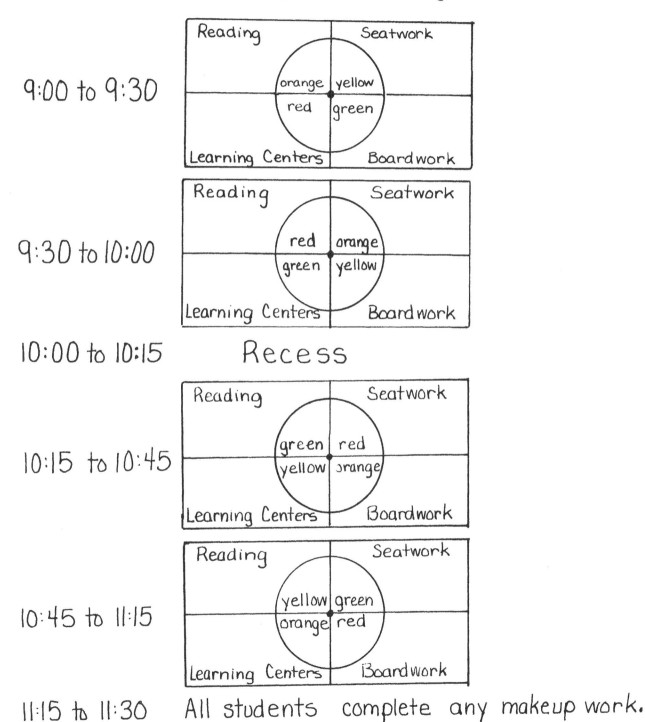

9:00 to 9:30

Reading	Seatwork
orange	yellow
red	green
Learning Centers	Boardwork

9:30 to 10:00

Reading	Seatwork
red	orange
green	yellow
Learning Centers	Boardwork

10:00 to 10:15   Recess

10:15 to 10:45

Reading	Seatwork
green	red
yellow	orange
Learning Centers	Boardwork

10:45 to 11:15

Reading	Seatwork
yellow	green
orange	red
Learning Centers	Boardwork

11:15 to 11:30   All students complete any makeup work.

Turn the color wheel clockwise after you have completed one-half hour with a reading group. The groups rotate until they have completed the four areas (approximately two hours every morning).

A "makeup" time of approximately fifteen minutes is held after all four reading groups are finished. Children with incomplete work (which has been placed in a box labeled "Makeup") have the opportunity to complete their work. The other children use this time for games, books, and so on.

The afternoon schedule consists of whole-group activities: math, writing, social studies, science, gym, art, phonics, and so on.

ADVANTAGES OF USING LEARNING CENTERS

There are many advantages of teaching reading simultaneously with learning centers, seatwork, and boardwork. These include:

1. A quiet atmosphere is established for teaching reading.
2. Each learning center theme reinforces skills in many disciplines, such as communication, math, science, computers, art, and so on.
3. The students gain independence as they participate daily at a learning center.
4. The students develop long-term memory skills.
5. The students learn how to pace themselves to complete each work area in a thirty-minute time block.
6. The teacher has one-to-one contact with each child daily.
7. Learning center themes change every eight school days.
8. The students are motivated by the theme and so is the teacher.
9. The learning center system is manageable by one teacher.

HOW TO MAKE A COLOR WHEEL FEATURING FOUR
READING GROUPS

Make a color wheel out of posterboard for your classroom as shown here.

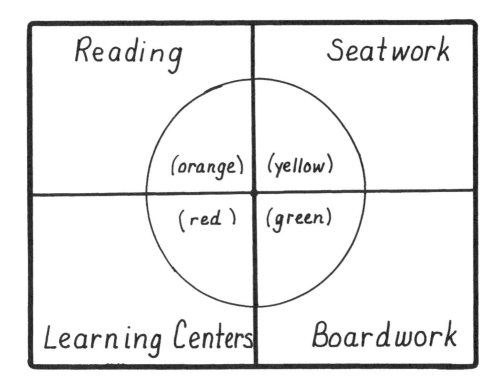

The color arrangement of the circular piece depends on the order in which you want the four groups to move to the four areas. Since the order of the groups may vary from year to year, you may need to make additional color wheels. Use a brass fastener to connect the center of the color wheel to the center of the posterboard and attach any additional color wheels onto the brass fastener on the *back* of the posterboard for future use.

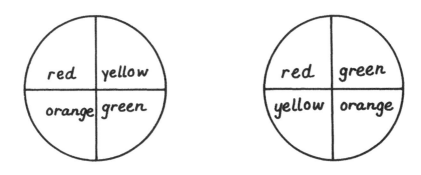

Alternative Group Suggestions

1. You could have four groups of children going to five learning centers (two children per learning center in each group). Learning centers would then be changed at the end of five days.

2. If your students go to another teacher for reading instruction, you could group them according to math ability or in other small groups.

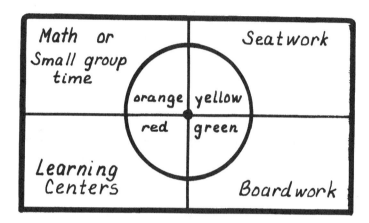

3. You may want to have three reading groups going to the four areas of the room. You would then have one area of the room vacant per color wheel rotation. You would be able to work individually with students when the reading area is vacant as pictured on the color wheel.

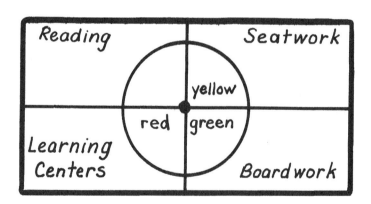

4. You may prefer to have five groups moving to five room areas for reading, reading workbooks, seatwork, boardwork, and learning centers.

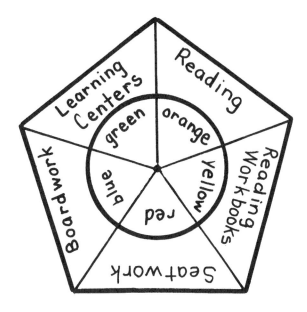

HOW TO SET UP THE CLASSROOM INTO FOUR AREAS

The arrangement of the furniture in the classroom is important for creating a good learning environment. The room should be set up to give the students the freedom to move physically and academically from one area to another.

Prior to the first day of school, arrange the furniture to create four areas: seatwork, boardwork, reading, and learning centers. It is easier to develop a set routine in the beginning weeks of the school year than to rearrange the classroom when you start the four-group movement (approximately three weeks later).

The main area of the classroom should be divided into two parts, one for seatwork and one for boardwork. Bookcases, storage boxes, and the like can be placed in a long row to serve as a main divider between the seatwork and boardwork areas (see Floor Plan A).

The desks in the boardwork area will usually face a chalkboard, from which the students will be copying your assignments. Some ideas for assignments are the Enrichment and Takeoff activities given in each language arts unit chapter. These activities include creative writing, riddles, tongue twisters, and spelling, as well as others.

In the seatwork area, the desks do not need to face the chalkboard. Seatwork activities may include phonics, mathematics, social studies, reading workbook pages, and so on. Many of the Enrichment activities given in each language arts unit are also suitable for seatwork.

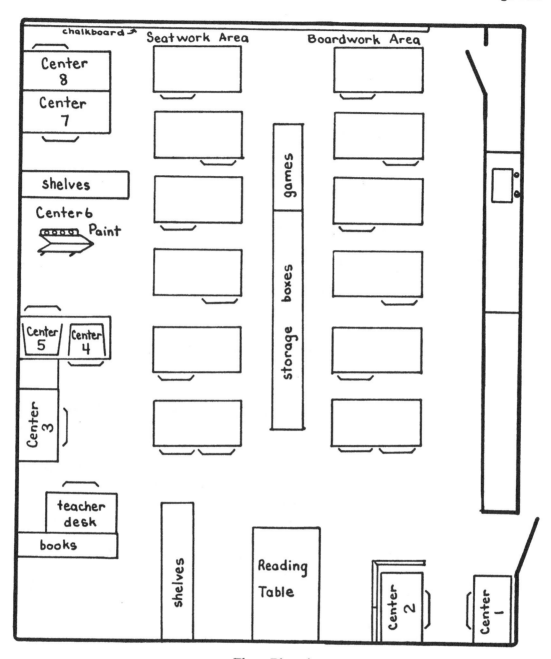

Floor Plan A

Cardboard can be used as an effective divider if bookcases are unavailable. Several thin, 3½-foot square pieces can be placed between a row of seatwork desks and a row of boardwork desks. When the children are seated, they cannot see over the top of the cardboard. This eliminates interaction between the two groups. (If you have taller children, you may want higher pieces of cardboard.) The cardboard pieces can easily be removed for whole-group activities, such as parties, cooking, and art projects (see Floor Plan B).

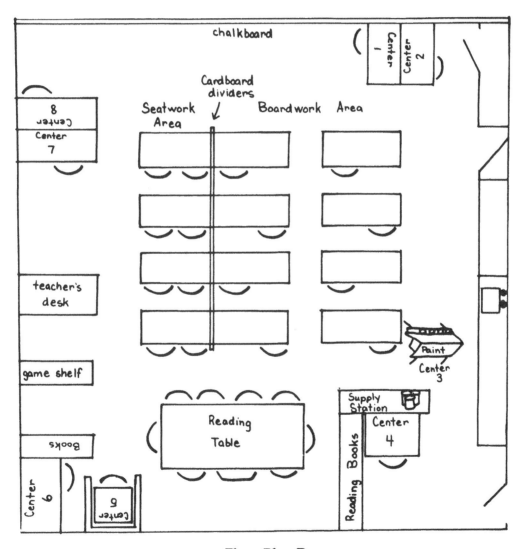

Floor Plan B

HOW TO ASSIGN DESKS

An important factor to consider in room arrangement is the assignment of desks. There is a method for seating that allows for maximum mobility in the classroom: The children do not have any assigned desks; only the tops of the desks are used, not the insides. (You may prefer to turn the desks so the open ends are away from the seated children.)

Each child needs a shoe box or similar box for his or her pencils, crayons, scissors, and paste. (You can tape a laminated tagboard name card to the lid.) The shoe boxes are stored on a bookshelf that is easily accessible to the children. When a child enters the room each morning, he or she puts the shoe box on an empty seatwork or boardwork desk. The child uses this desk before school and during whole-group activities. When the child moves with his or her group to learning centers, seatwork, and boardwork, he or she brings the shoe box. During reading, the shoe box is put on the bookshelf.

You may prefer to have each child use a permanently assigned desk before school and during the whole-group activities of the day. In order to accommodate the mobility of the four groups to seatwork, boardwork, learning centers, and reading, all the desktops can be shared by everyone. (You may need to establish a rule that everyone works on desktops only.)

If desks are not permanently assigned, you may need to devise alternative storage areas such as bookshelves or boxes for textbooks, workbooks, library books, and so on.

HOW TO MAKE A DESK DIVIDER

Materials Needed

Three pieces of 16″ × 18″ cardboard

2 yards of 3″-wide duct tape or clear self-stick vinyl

4 yards of 18″-wide woodgrain or solid-color self-stick vinyl (bold patterns and colors may be distracting for some students).

Scissors

Procedure

1. Lay the three pieces of cardboard on the floor or table about ½″ apart. Wrap the duct tape or vinyl strips around the edges of the cardboard pieces A and B, and C and D (see the illustration). The duct tape acts as a hinge while joining all three cardboard pieces to make the divider.

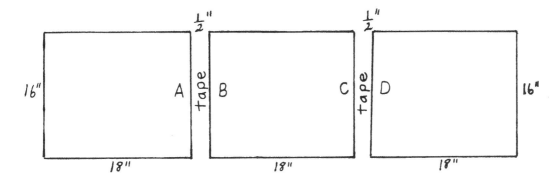

2. Lay the divider flat on the floor or table. Cover both the front and back sides of the divider with the woodgrain or solid-color self-stick vinyl.

3. For easy handling and storage, fold piece A over BC and piece D over A.

How to Use

The desk divider can be used effectively on an individual child's desk to block out any classroom distractions. (Children frequently choose to put a divider on their own desk because they know when they need one.) The desk divider is an ideal way to create two separate, quiet, independent work areas on a desk or table that seats two children. It is especially helpful to use the desk dividers during the seatwork period of the day.

- Two desk dividers can be placed on a table to create space for two separate learning centers (see Illustration A). Desk dividers can also be placed on the reading table to separate children working independently on tests or workbook pages, as shown in Illustration B.

You might also place a desk divider on a learning center table. The direction file folder, material envelopes, pictures, and the like can be attached to the divider with clothespins (see Illustration C).

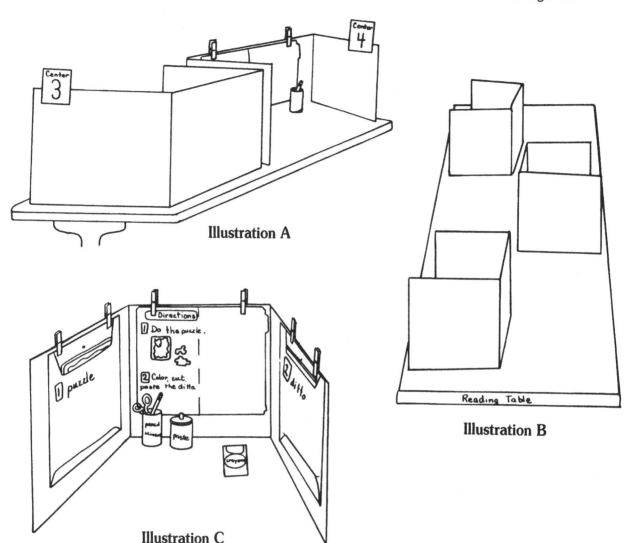

Illustration A

Illustration B

Illustration C

HOW TO KEEP TRACK OF EACH CHILD AT LEARNING CENTERS

Duplicate a center marker for each child (as pictured on page 13). Write the child's name on the marker after the marker has been duplicated.

Sort the markers into the four groups (red, orange, yellow, and green). Circle a different number on each child's marker in the red group with a marking pen. (In this way, each child in the red groups starts at a different learning center). Circle the numbers on the markers for the orange, yellow, and green groups in the same way.

Pass out the markers to each child to color and cut out. (It is helpful to have each child color his or her marker the color of the group, especially with the initial set of learning centers.)

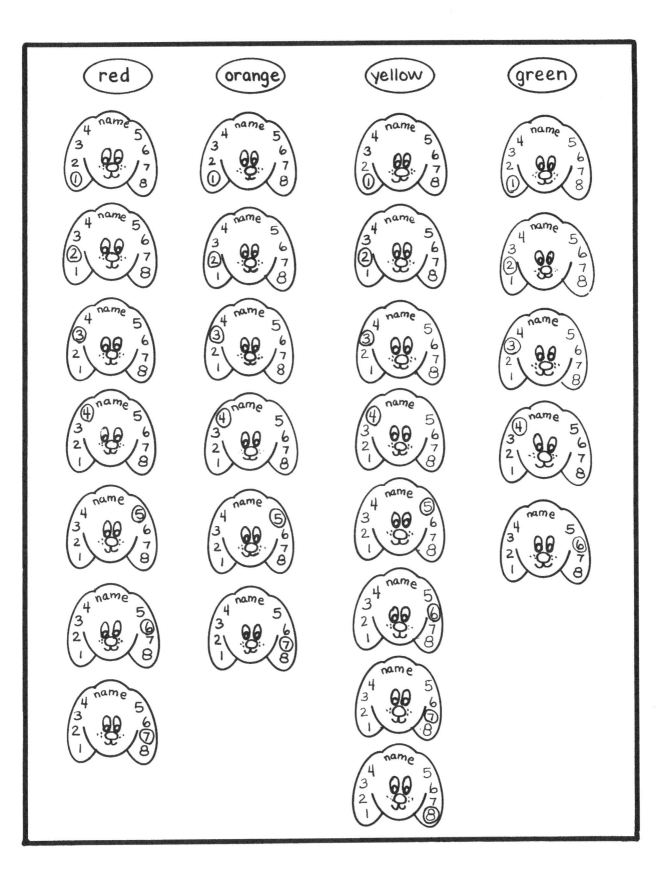

After the children have colored and cut out their markers, staple the markers in four groups on a bulletin board or divider. The markers should be near the reading area since the children move there after they finish the learning centers.

When a student has finished a learning center, he or she moves with his or her group to the reading area. The student finds his or her marker on the bulletin board, and using a marking pen puts an X on the number of the learning center just finished. Then he or she circles the next number in clockwise order. This is the number of the learning center at which he or she will work the following day. The student continues this pattern daily until all learning centers (one per day) have been completed. In the following example, the student would do a total of eight learning centers during an eight-day period.

If a child is absent, the teacher marks "Ab" next to the number of that child's learning center. Then the teacher circles the following day's center number. The learning centers missed due to absences are *not* made up. This is essential in keeping one child per learning center.

HOW TO EVALUATE THE LEARNING CENTER ACTIVITIES

When a group of students rotates to the reading area, they bring their completed learning center work to be graded. A variety of evaluation techniques may be used. One method enables both the student and the teacher to give input into the evaluation. Quality of work, following directions, ways to improve, and so on, are discussed. The evaluation is based on a joint student–teacher decision.

As an added incentive, the students who do very good learning center work are encouraged to display it in the hallway. The graded papers may be placed in a box, and at a prearranged time the students can put them up in the hallway. The papers are changed daily, thus enabling a child to have only one paper per day in the hallway.

Some ideas for a hallway display area include using a bulletin board or a tack strip, taping papers to the wall, or hanging projects on a wire or string from the ceiling. Since the display will feature learning center work throughout the year, you may want to make a permanent sign such as "Room 7's Learning Centers are About . . ." You would only need to change the title of the learning center theme on your sign, such as "Dr. Seuss and His Friends," as shown in the illustration.

HOW TO INTRODUCE A NEW SET OF LEARNING CENTERS TO THE ENTIRE CLASS

1. Seat all the children on the floor near the first learning center. (After you have finished the directions for the first learning center, the group continues to move with you to each additional learning center. This may take thirty to forty-five minutes to explain eight learning centers. No additional directions will be necessary for the eight-day period.) It is helpful to explain the centers in the afternoon prior to the day you are beginning a new set of centers.

2. Explain the directions in consecutive order at each learning center.

3. Demonstrate any special equipment, such as filmstrip previewer or computer, at the learning center.

4. Discuss the proper care of materials, such as fragile items. If materials were borrowed from a media center, you may want to emphasize special handling.

5. Indicate any activities that need to be checked by you before the child leaves the learning center, such as flannelboard, bulletin board, chalkboard, or floor manipulative activities.

6. Discuss clean-up rules. If the learning center is disorderly when a child goes to it, he or she should get the child who preceded him or her to clean up.

7. Allow time for questions at each learning center. By explaining a set of learning centers thoroughly, you will eliminate daily interruptions. (A child may quietly ask another person in his or her group for additional help with directions when he or she is working at a learning center.)

HOW TO EXPLAIN LEARNING CENTERS TO PARENTS

The following letter is sent home on the first day learning centers are used (approximately the third week of September). Since many parents work and are unable to visit the school during the day, an evening meeting should be arranged to discuss the centers with parents (the letter on page 19 is also sent). Do this after you have begun using learning centers, usually some time in October.

All About Learning Centers

Date _____

Dear Parent,

During the first few weeks of school, I have been reviewing the skills your child has learned in the past. The children have been given a variety of tests.

Today we began a new morning routine that we will follow all year. The children have been divided into four groups based on reading ability. The four groups are red, green, yellow, and orange. The children move every half hour to four areas of the classroom to do seatwork, boardwork, reading, and learning center activities.

A color wheel (in the center of this diagram) helps us keep track of where we are working:

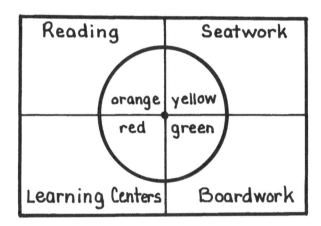

In this diagram, the orange group is working with me at the reading area, the yellow group is doing seatwork (math and phonics papers), the green group is at the boardwork area (copying some type of work from the chalkboard), and the red group is working at eight different learning centers (one child per learning center). At the end of one half hour, the color wheel is turned clockwise and all the groups move to the next area. The groups continue to move in this way until each group has completed all four areas.

A makeup time (approximately fifteen minutes) is given after the children have completed all four areas. This enables all the children to finish their morning work. In the afternoon we have whole-group activities: math, social studies, phonics, spelling, art, handwriting, and so on.

Participation in learning centers will be a new experience for many of our children. I have prepared activities for eight individual learning centers covering the following skills: math, art, social studies, science, reading, listening, handwriting, and coordination.

There are several reasons why I am teaching with learning centers: (1) The classroom is quieter; (2) a structured routine is followed daily; (3) the children learn to follow directions; (4) independent study habits are established; (5) the children can pace themselves to work for thirty minutes; (6) the children learn to evaluate themselves; and (7) a wide variety of subjects provides experiences in learning something new, reinforcing old skills, or developing creativity.

During the next eight school days the learning centers will be based on the theme _____ . If you have books, records, or games about this learning center topic, please share them. (Please be sure that your child's name is on any item sent to school.) If you are interested in seeing our learning centers in action, please contact me to arrange an appointment. I am looking forward to seeing you.

The beginning weeks of learning centers may present some new adjustments. We will have a routine established within a week. Thank you for your support.

Sincerely,

_____

Your child's teacher

Learning Centers Evening Meeting

October _____

Dear Parent,

    Since many parents are unable to visit the classroom during the school day, I would like to invite you and your child to a group meeting. The meeting will be held in Room _____ at the _____ School on _____ at _____ P.M. It will last approximately one hour.

    The meeting will consist of the following:

1. A brief presentation of the learning centers approach that we are using daily in our classroom.
2. A question-and-answer period.
3. An opportunity for you and your child to visit our room to see learning centers.

    I appreciate the support that you have given me this year. I would like to know how many people plan to attend the meeting. Please return the following note by _____ .

Sincerely,

_____
Your child's teacher

_____
Your child's name

Please check one of the following:
_____ We will be able to attend the meeting on _____ .
        The number planning to attend is _____ .
_____ We will not be able to attend the meeting.

_____
Parent's signature

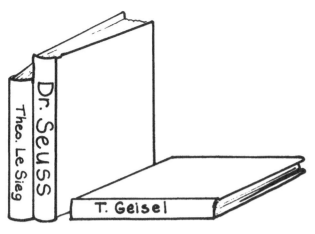

Dr. Seuss and His Friends

Bears

Language Arts Learning Centers

Dogs

American Tall Tales and Legends

Dr. Seuss
and His Friends

Ten apples Up on Top

people House

Lorax

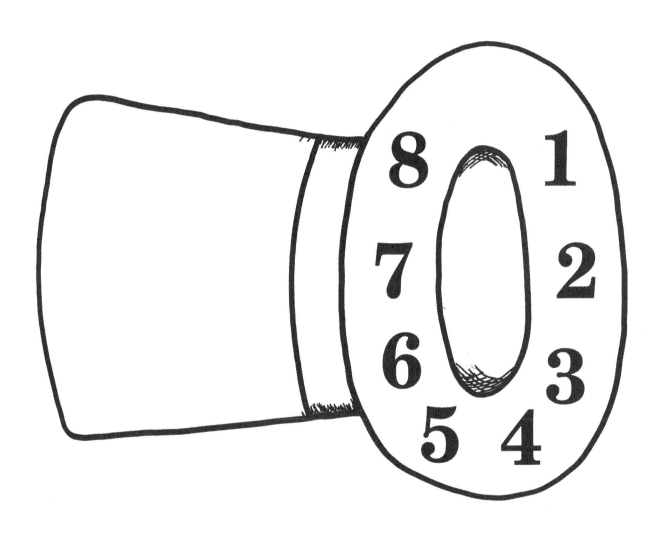

"Dr. Seuss and His Friends"
Center Marker

Dr. Seuss on the Loose!

Date _____

Dear Parent,

Watch out! You may find Dr. Seuss on the loose in our classroom during the next two weeks.

"Dr. Seuss and His Friends" is the theme for our language arts learning centers. Each center will feature a different book written by Theodor Geisel for your child to read and enjoy. Mr. Geisel has written many wonderful children's books under the pen names Dr. Seuss and Theo. Le Sieg.

The *Ten Apples up on Top!* center will emphasize number words. Your child will match number-word cards with apples on the bulletin board.

At the *Cat in the Hat* center, your child will make a bow-tie matching game. He or she may want to play this game at home with someone in your family.

Your child will have an opportunity to use a typewriter or computer at the *Dr. Seuss A B C* center. You may want to encourage your child to use a typewriter or computer at home to develop keyboard skills.

Listen to your child read a tongue twister which he or she will write at the *Fox in Socks* center. You may want to read and tape-record some tongue twisters with your child.

Using the book *In a People House* as a reference, your child will make his or her own rhyming-word book. Encourage your child to read his or her book to a younger friend.

You are welcome to send in Dr. Seuss books, puzzles, records, tapes, and so on, during the next two weeks. Please be sure your child's name is on any item brought to class.

Thank you for your continued support.

Sincerely,

_____
Your child's teacher

HOTLINE FROM

Parent TO School

Date _____

Dear Parent,

    I would appreciate any feedback you or your child may have regarding the "Dr. Seuss and His Friends" learning centers: *Ten Apples up on Top, The Lorax, The Cat in the Hat, Dr. Seuss's A B C, In a People House, McElligot's Pool, Fox in Socks,* and *Wacky Wednesday.*
    Please use this page for comments and return it to me by _____ .

Sincerely,

_____

Your child's teacher

Date _____

Dear _____ ,

"DR. SEUSS AND HIS FRIENDS" LEARNING CENTERS LIST

These learning centers feature books written by Theodor Geisel (Dr. Seuss and Theo. Le Sieg).

Ten Apples up on Top! Center

(A bulletin board is used with this center)

Skills Reading, using reference materials, math, fine-motor coordination

Activities

1. Match number-word cards and apples on the bulletin board.
2. Complete the number-word work on the Student Activity Page.

Cat in the Hat Center (Open-Ended Activity)

Skills Reading, speaking, fine-motor coordination, teacher's choice

Activities

1. Make a tie game using the Student Activity Page.
2. Play the tie game with a friend.

McElligot's Pool Center

Skills Reading, creative writing, fine-motor coordination, art

Activities

1. Make fish and other objects for the mural. Paste the objects onto the mural.
2. Write and illustrate a story on the Student Activity Page.

Dr. Seuss's A B C Center

Skills Reading, keyboarding, computer, using reference materials, spelling

Activities

1. Type the lowercase and uppercase letters of the alphabet and your name on the Student Activity Page.
2. Type and illustrate words from your favorite page in the book on the back of the Student Activity Page.

Fox in Socks Center

Skills Reading, listening, speaking, using reference materials, fine-motor coordination

Activities

1. Listen to the cassette tape of the book.
2. Write a tongue twister on the chalkboard and the Student Activity Page.

Wacky Wednesday **Center**

Skills Reading, math, creating, using reference materials, computer, fine-motor coordination, spelling

Activities

1. Use references to write the name of the month, year, days of the week, and numbers of the days on the student activity page calendar. Paste the calendar onto paper.
2. Illustrate the events of a "Wacky Wednesday" on the calendar.

The Lorax **Center**

Skills Reading, creating, fine-motor coordination, science

Activities

1. Observe the slides of pollution under a microscope.
2. Draw a picture about the land of the Lorax. Paint the picture with a purple paint wash.

In a People House **Center**

Skills Reading, using reference materials, spelling, art, fine-motor coordination

Activities

1. Assemble student activity pages into a book.
2. Write and illustrate rhyming words in the book.

"DR. SEUSS AND HIS FRIENDS" CENTER MARKER

Distribute copies of the hat marker (refer to page 23) to the students. The students can color and cut out their markers, then place them near the "Dr. Seuss and His Friends" learning centers.

TEACHER'S DIRECTIONS FOR *TEN APPLES UP ON TOP!* CENTER

Skills Reading, using reference materials, math, fine-motor coordination

Materials Needed

　　Book: Le Sieg, Theo., *Ten Apples up on Top!* New York: Random House, 1961
　　Bulletin board
　　Copies of Student Activity Page (see page 31)
　　Teacher-made set of apples
　　Teacher-made set of number word cards
　　Teacher-made number-word reference chart
　　Thumbtacks and container
　　Crayons
　　Pencil

Materials Preparation

　　1. Prepare a bulletin board as pictured.

　　2. To make the set of apples, draw thirty or more apples on posterboard or construction paper. Cut out the apples, laminate them, and put them into the basket on the bulletin board.

　　3. For the set of number-word cards, make a set of ten cards with the appropriate number-word skill you wish to reinforce written on them. Laminate

the cards and put them in the number-word envelope on the bulletin board. A skill ideas for younger students is to have them match ten number words (*one* through *ten*) with the approriate number of apples tacked above the heads on the bulletin board. Older students can match addition of three equation cards such as *one + two + three* with the appropriate number of apples tacked above the heads on the bulletin board. They can also match multiplication of number words of the three's time table, such as *three × one, three × two,* and so on, with the appropriate number of apples tacked above the heads on the bulletin board.

4. Prior to duplicating the Student Activity Page, write in the appropriate number-word math skill you wish to reinforce on the apples, such as one + two + three and so on.

5. Make a reference chart of the number words to display at this center such as 1 one, 2 two, and so on.

Directions for File Folder Activities

Activity 1

The younger student tacks number-word cards next to the heads on the bulletin board. Then he or she tacks the appropriate number of apples above the heads to match the number-word cards. The older student takes an equation card and tacks the apples above the heads to illustrate the equation. He or she continues until all cards have been used.

Activity 2

The student completes the work on the Student Activity Page per your directions.

Takeoff

Plan an apple tasting party. Encourage each child to bring in one apple of a specific variety (for example, Golden Delicious, Red Delicious, Jonathan, Macintosh, Spartan). You or the children could slice, core, and serve the apples. (Use an apple slicer if one is available.) The children can eat and compare the different kinds of apples (color, taste, texture, size). You may want to graph the comparisons.

Ten Apples Up On Top!

by Theo. LeSieg

1 Match the cards and the apples.

2

Do the page.

Ten Apples up on Top!
File Folder Directions

name _____

How many apples up on top ?

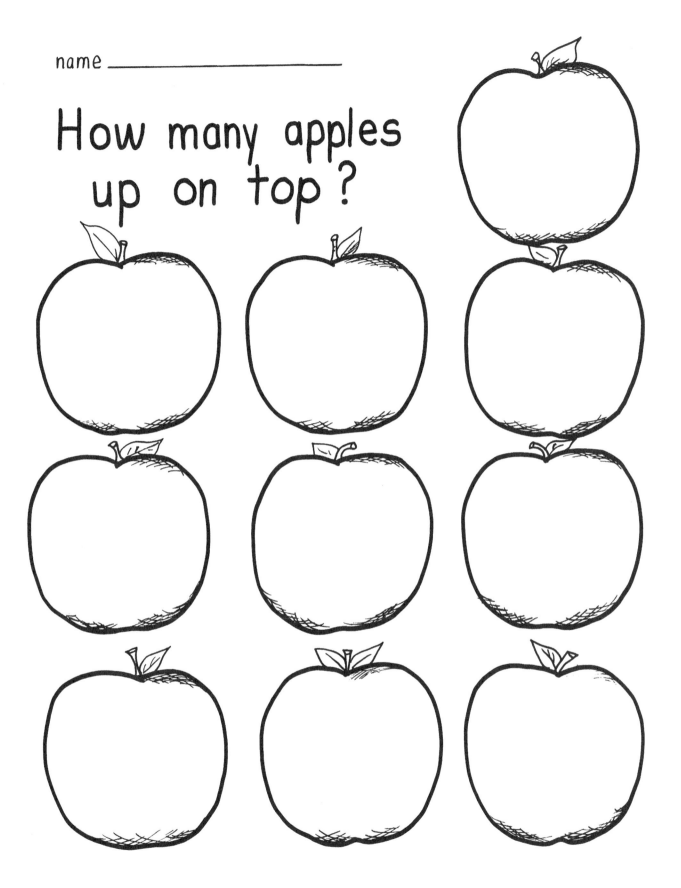

Ten Apples up on Top!
Student Activity Page

TEACHER'S DIRECTIONS FOR *THE CAT IN THE HAT* CENTER

Skills Reading, speaking, fine-motor coordination, teacher's choice

Materials Needed

Book: Seuss, Dr., *The Cat in the Hat,* New York: Random House, 1957
Copies of Student Activity Page (see page 35) on heavy paper
Teacher-made tie matching game
Teacher-made reference chart
One small envelope per student
Pencil
Scissors

Materials Preparation

1. To make the tie matching game use a copy of the Student Activity Page to reinforce or review a skill. Some ideas are upper- and lowercase letters, color words and colors, number words and numerals, contractions, opposite words, and compound words. Write the words or numerals on the ties and cut them out. Then cut each tie apart differently to make the game self-checking.

2. Laminate the game and provide a container for it.

3. Make a reference chart by writing words or numerals on a copy of the Student Activity Page.

Directions for File Folder Activities

Activity 1

The student makes a tie game of his or her own, referring to your game or reference chart. He or she puts the game in the envelope.

Activity 2

The student may play the game with a friend.

Takeoff

1. The students may list ten or more pairs of rhyming words found in *The Cat in the Hat*. You may want to duplicate the following words for younger students: *cat, sunny, say, wish, fall, cake, fox, box, hook, hit, thump, fear,* and *kicks*. (The younger student would list a rhyming word for each of the above words, such as: *cat, hat; sunny, funny; say, day; wish, fish; fall, ball; cake, rake*).

2. Read aloud *The Cat in the Hat* to the class. Then discuss the sequence of the events of the book. Some ideas are
   a. What were Sally and her brother doing at the beginning of the story?
   b. What happened after Sally and her brother heard a bump?
   c. What tricks did the Cat in the Hat do on the ball?
   d. What did the Things like to do?
   e. Who cleaned up the mess?
   f. What happened at the end of the story?
   The students may want to illustrate the sequence of events or a favorite part of the book.

3. You may also want to read Dr. Seuss's *The Cat in the Hat Comes Back* (New York: Random House, 1958).

The Cat in the Hat
by Dr. Seuss

1 Make a game.

2 Play it
with a friend.

The Cat in the Hat
File Folder Directions

Tie Matching Game

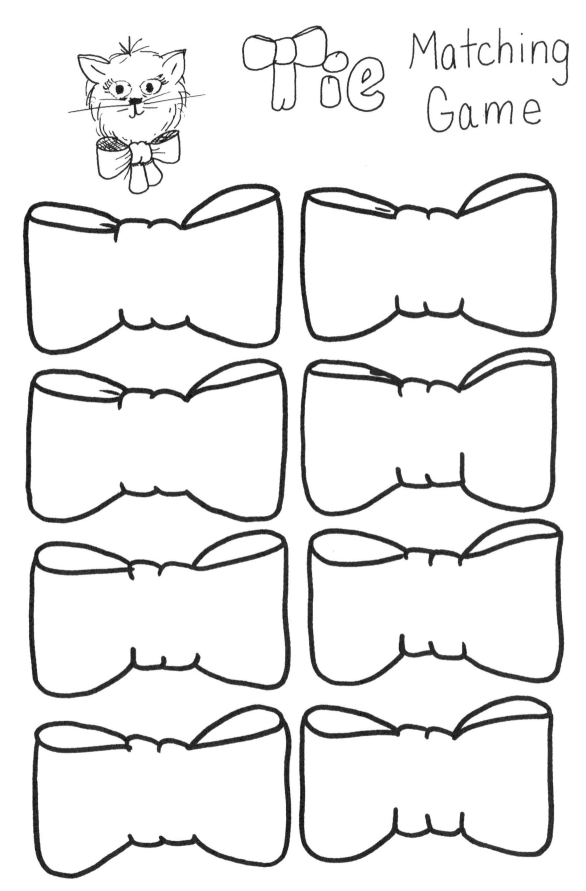

The Cat in the Hat
Student Activity Page

TEACHER'S DIRECTIONS FOR *McELLIGOT'S POOL* CENTER

Skills Reading, creative writing, fine-motor coordination, art

Materials needed

    Book: Seuss, Dr., *McElligot's Pool,* New York: Random House, 1947

    Copies of Student Activity Page (see page 39)

    Pencil

    Crayons

    Scissors

    Paste

    Construction paper in assorted colors and sizes

Materials Preparation

    1. Prepare an area such as a bulletin board, the floor, or a table with large paper for a mural. Prepare a background with a large pool, hills, and so on, similar to the book. Or have the students do this.

    2. Determine the number of fish you want each student to make for the mural. You may also want the students to make junk objects, people, animals, and so on, for the mural.

Directions for File Folder Activities

    Activity 1

    The student uses crayons, scissors, and construction paper to make fish and other objects for the mural. He or she pastes the objects onto the mural.

    Activity 2

    The student writes a creative story on the Student Activity Page, for example, "If I Went Fishing in McElligot's Pool . . ." He or she illustrates the story.

Takeoff

1. Read *McElligot's Pool* aloud to the class. Discuss the kinds of fish in the story. List all the fish on chart paper. The students may copy the list of fish in alphabetical order.

2. The students may use references such as encyclopedias, dictionaries, and fish books to find the fish described in *McElligot's Pool*. They may list the fish in categories such as "real" and "imaginary."

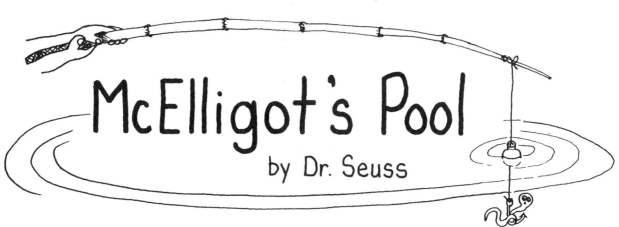

McElligot's Pool
by Dr. Seuss

1. Make fish and objects for the mural.

2. Write a story.

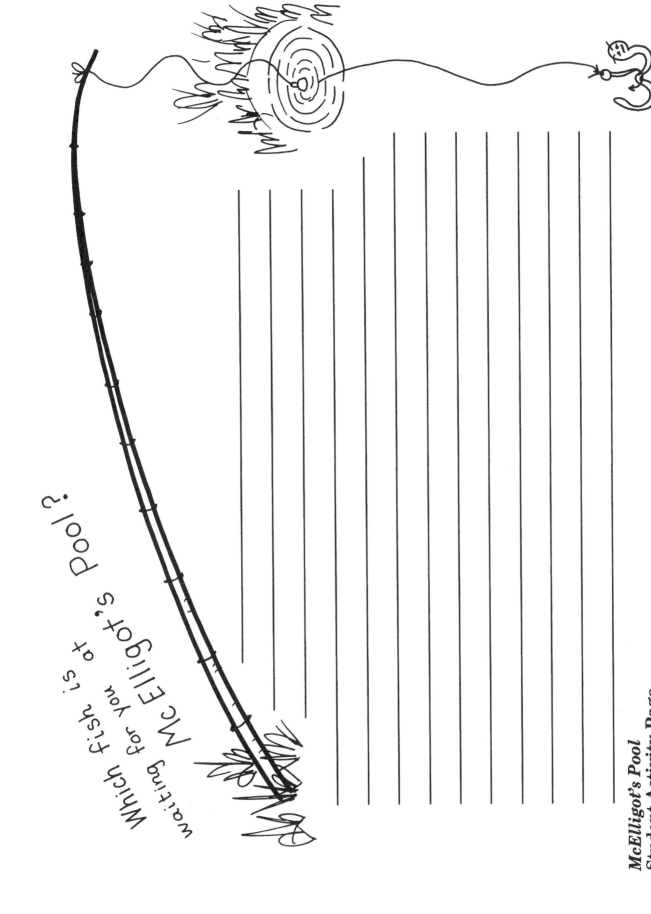

Which fish is at McElligot's Pool waiting for you?

TEACHER'S DIRECTIONS FOR *DR. SEUSS'S A B C* CENTER

Skills Reading, keyboarding/computer, using reference materials, spelling

Materials Needed

Book: Seuss, Dr., *Dr. Seuss's A B C* (Random House, 1963)
Copies of Student Activity Page (see page 43)
Old typewriter or computer and printer
Pencil

Materials Preparation

1. Instruct the students on the proper way to load the Student Activity Page into the typewriter carriage. If this is the students' first experience with classroom typing, assure the students that mistakes will be acceptable.

2. Encourage the students to proofread their typing *after* the paper is removed from the typewriter. They may cross out any errors or write in missing letters (no erasing is allowed).

3. If a typewriter is not available, these options may work:
    a. Use a computer and printer with an appropriate beginner word-processing program. The student may use the Student Activity Page for directions. You may want to display a completed printout sheet for a reference.
    b. Use a stamp letter set and ink pad to print the letters.

Directions for File Folder Activities

Activity 1

The student types the lowercase and uppercase letters of the alphabet on the Student Activity Page. Then he or she types his or her name.

Activity 2

The student types the words from his or her favorite page in the book on the back of the Student Activity Page. He or she may illustrate his or her favorite page on the back, too.

Takeoff

1. The student may type a "Dr. Seuss Word List." He or she could type the letters of the alphabet in vertical order (triple spaced) on paper. Then, referring to *Dr. Seuss's A B C*, the student could type one or more words for each letter of the alphabet.

2. You may want to make a class alphabet book. Each student could write the name of a character from a Dr. Seuss book and illustrate it on a page. (You would need to assign a specific letter to each child.) The book could become a traveling book. (See the last section, "Enjoying Language Arts.")

Dr. Seuss's ABC
by Dr. Seuss

1. Type the abc's and your name.

2. Type the words from your favorite page on the back.

Dr. Seuss's A B C
File Folder Directions

ABC Fun

1. Type the lowercase letters.
a b c d e f g h i j k l m n o p q r s t u v w x y z

2. Type the uppercase letters.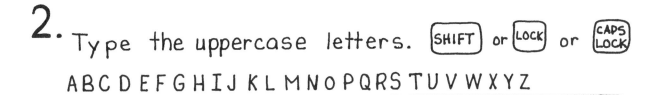
A B C D E F G H I J K L M N O P Q R S T U V W X Y Z

3. Type your first and last name.

Dr. Seuss's A B C
Student Activity Page

TEACHER'S DIRECTIONS FOR *FOX IN SOCKS* CENTER

Skills Reading, listening, speaking, using reference materials, fine-motor coordination

Materials Needed

   Book: Seuss, Dr., *Fox in Socks,* New York: Random House, 1965
   Copies of Student Activity Page (see page 47)
   Teacher-made tongue twister cards and container
   Chalkboard
   Chalk
   Tape recorder
   Cassette tape
   Pencil
   Crayons

Materials Preparation

   1. Prepare a cassette tape of the book.

   2. Make a collection of tongue twister cards. Select some of the tongue twisters from the book to write on index cards.

   3. Laminate the cards and provide a container for them.

Directions for File Folder Activities

   Activity 1

   The student listens to the cassette tape of the book. (You may want to encourage the student to play the tape an additional time enabling him or her to read the book aloud.)

   Activity 2

   The student selects a tongue twister from the card collection and writes it on the chalkboard. He or she writes a tongue twister on the student activity page. (The tongue twister may be an original creation or one selected from the card collection.) The student may color the Student Activity Page.

Takeoff

1. Read aloud *Fox in Socks* or another Dr. Seuss book entitled *Oh Say Can You Say?* (New York: Random House, 1979). Help the students learn some tongue twisters, then tape-record the students saying them.

2. Write a different tongue twister on the chalkboard each day for a few weeks. The students may copy the tongue twisters and compile them into their own books. Encourage the students to read the books to their families or another class. (See "Enjoying Language Arts" at the end of this book.)

Fox in Socks
by Dr. Seuss

1 Listen to the book.

2 Write a tongue twister on the board and on the page.

Fox in Socks
Student Activity Page

TEACHER'S DIRECTIONS FOR *WACKY WEDNESDAY* CENTER

Skills Reading, math, creating, using reference materials, computer, fine-motor coordination, spelling

Materials Needed

Book: Le Sieg, Theo., *Wacky Wednesday,* New York: Random House, 1974

Copies of Student Activity Page (see page 51)

Teacher-made reference chart or references (dictionary or pictionary)

Old calendars (optional)

12″ × 18″ construction paper

Computer and printer (optional)

Pencil

Crayons

Paste

Materials Preparation

1. Make a reference chart of the month, year, and days of the week for younger students. Optional: Provide references such as a dictionary, pictionary, or an old calendar (with the month and days of the week on it).

2. Older students can create a calendar on a computer and printer if available.

3. Prior to beginning this center make a collection of numbers for use by older students. You or the students can cut the numbers from three or four old calendars and place them in a container at this center.

Directions for File Folder Activities

Activity 1

The student uses references to write the name of the month, the year, and the days of the week (unscrambling the names of the days of the week at the bottom of the Student Activity Page) on the Student Activity Page. The younger student writes the numbers of the days of the month on the Student Activity Page calendar. The older student sorts the collection of numbers and pastes the numbers of the days of the month in order on the Student Activity Page calendar.

The student pastes the Student Activity Page calendar onto the lower half of the construction paper as pictured in the File Folder Directions.

Activity 2

The student uses crayons to illustrate the events of a Wacky Wednesday on the construction paper above the calendar.

Takeoff

1. The students may draw ten or more things that are wacky referring to *Wacky Wednesday*. Older students may describe twenty things that are wacky and illustrate them referring to *Wacky Wednesday*.

2. Celebrate a Wacky Wednesday in your classroom. Students can help plan the events in advance. You or the students may write letters to parents explaining your Wacky Wednesday agenda. Some ideas are
   a. Wear clothing such as hats, shirts, sweaters, and so on, backward.
   b. Read books backward (start at the end and read to the beginning).
   c. Write events of the day in journals.
   d. Write spelling words in scrambled order on the chalkboard. The students would unscramble the words and list them in the correct order.
   e. Write days of the week and months of the year in mixed order. The students would list them in correct order.
   f. Make and serve upside-down cake.

Sunday Monday Tuesday WEDNESDAY Thursday Friday Saturday

Wacky Wednesday
by Theo. LeSieg

1 Make a calendar.

2 Draw what might happen on Wacky WEDNESDAY!

Paste

Wacky Wednesday
File Folder Directions

month: _____   year: _____

yrdifa   ddeaynuse   yusadn   rasaytdu   aeuydst   yadomn   ruhaydst

* Each day of the week must be capitalized. *

Wacky Wednesday
Student Activity Page

TEACHER'S DIRECTIONS FOR *THE LORAX* CENTER

Skills Reading, creating, fine-motor coordination, science

Materials Needed

Book: Seuss, Dr., *The Lorax,* New York: Random House, 1971

Microscope or hand magnifier

A collection of air pollution slides

Wax crayons

Purple paint (tempera or water color)

Paintbrush

Easel

Old shirt

Paper

Materials Preparation

1. Discuss air pollution with your students. If commercially prepared slides of air pollution are not available, you may wish to have the students look at a variety of water samples. You may want to include tap water, rain water, pond water, and so on. The students may want to record their observations.

2. When you introduce this center, draw a few objects from the book with wax crayons on paper. Then apply a diluted purple paint wash with a brush over the entire surface of the paper. Compare the purple paint wash to the darkened, pollution illustrations in the book.

Directions for File Folder Activities

Activity 1

The student observes the slides under a microscope or hand magnifier.

Activity 2

The student draws a picture about what the land of the Lorax looked like before the Once-ler came. Then he or she paints a purple paint wash over his or her picture.

Takeoff

1. Read *The Lorax* aloud to the class, then discuss it. Some suggestions are
   a. Who was the Once-ler?
   b. What was the land and water like before the Once-ler came?
   c. What was the land and water like at the end of the book?
   d. Why did the animals leave?
   e. What real animals are having the same problems now?
   f. Why did so many animals want Thneeds?
   g. Why did Thneeds, Inc., go out of business?
   h. What could the Once-ler have done to prevent the problem?
   i. What products come from trees?
   j. What can you do to help keep our environment a good place for people and animals to live?

2. The students may do creative writing after reading *The Lorax*. Some ideas are "If I had the last truffula seed . . .," "If I met the Once-ler . . .," "If I had a Whisper-ma-Phone . . .," "If I had a Thneed . . .," and so on. (You might compile the stories into a class traveling book, as described in "Enjoying Language Arts" at the end of this book.)

The Lorax
by Dr. Seuss

UNLESS   UNLESS

1 Look at the slides.

2 Draw a picture about <u>The Lorax.</u>

Then add the "pollution."

purple

The Lorax
File Folder Directions

TEACHER'S DIRECTIONS FOR *IN A PEOPLE HOUSE* CENTER

Skills Reading, using reference materials, spelling, art, fine-motor coordination

Materials Needed

Book: Le Sieg, Theo., *In a People House,* New York: Random House, 1972

Copies of Student Activity Pages (see pages 58 and 59)

Teacher-made book

Pencil

Crayons

Scissors

Stapler and staples

Materials Preparation

Make a book as pictured on the File Folder Directions Page, using copies of the Student Activity Pages. You will need to determine the number of pages per book (older students can do several):

a. The students will write and illustrate the pairs of rhyming words on adjacent pages referring to the *In a People House* book.

b. You may prefer to write rhyming word pairs on adjacent pages for younger students to copy, such as "chairs, stairs" or "chairs, s _ _ _ _ s" (the student writes the missing letters in the blanks, referring to *In a People House*). The student illustrates the rhyming word pairs.

Directions for File Folder Activities

Activity 1

The student assembles his or her book per your directions.

Activity 2

The student writes and illustrates rhyming words, referring to *In a People House.*

Takeoff

1. The students may list or illustrate words in categories, referring to *In a People House*. Some ideas are

Animals—mouse, Mr. Bird, goldfish, people

Food—banana, doughnuts, popcorn, peanuts, bread, butter

Furniture—bed, chairs, table, drawers, sink

Toys—roller skates, piano, ball, books, marbles, doll

Parts of a room—wall, floor, ceiling, door, stairs

Clothes—shirt, shoe, sock

Things that make noise—TV, telephone, bell, clock

2. The students may write and illustrate couplets. They may use words from *In a People House* as starters. Some suggestions are

    a. Bells ring
       On a string.

    b. Cats crash
       In the trash.

    c. Balls fall
       Off a wall.

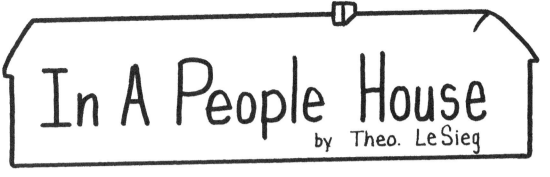

In A People House
by Theo. LeSieg

1 Make a book.

2 Write and illustrate rhyming words.

In a People House
File Folder Directions

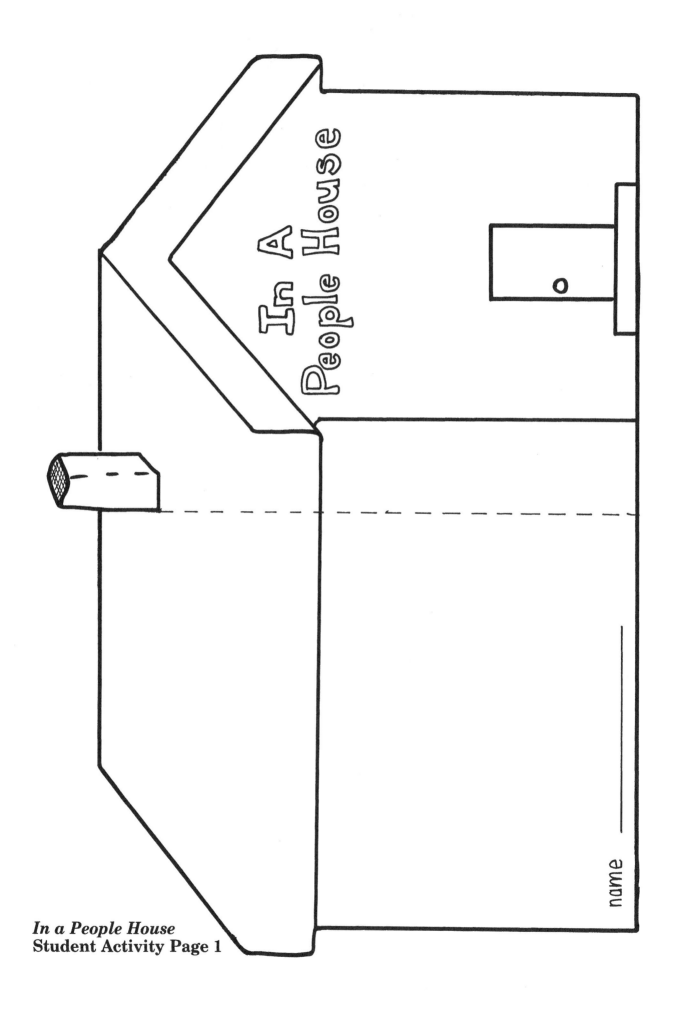

In A
People House

name _____

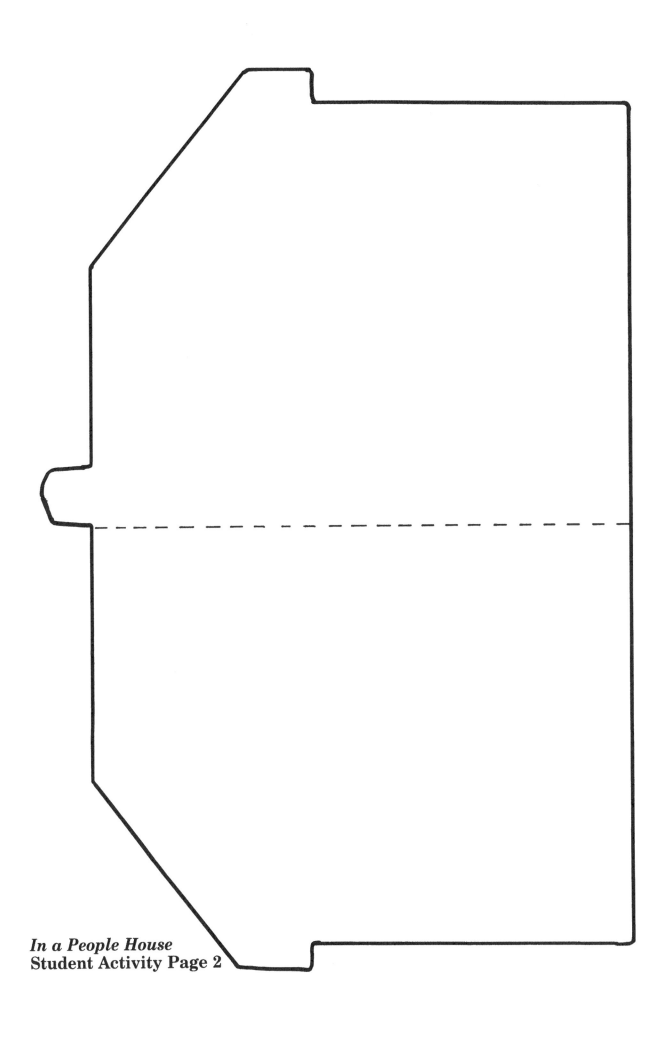

In a People House
Student Activity Page 2

Dr. Seuss

Enrichment Activities

Would you eat them in a train?

Grinch

500 Hats

TEACHER'S DIRECTIONS FOR "DR. SEUSS AND HIS FRIENDS" ENRICHMENT ACTIVITIES

"Dr. Seuss and His Friends" Group Activity

As a culminating activity to the Dr. Seuss language arts unit, schedule a Hat Day. Send the Hat Day letter or have the students write a letter to parents at least one week before Hat Day.

Prior to Hat Day, each student will choose a Dr. Seuss book. He or she will create a hat at home (or you may prefer to do this project at school) depicting a character or some aspect of the book. The student may make a hat out of scrap materials, such as paper bags, paper plates, construction paper, wallpaper, material scraps, beads, feathers, ribbons, and so on, or he or she may use an old hat of his or her own or a family member's hat. Some ideas are to attach ten apples (construction paper or scrap material) to a hat for *Ten Apples up on Top!,* attach fish and other objects to a hat for *McElligot's Pool,* make a socks hat for the *Fox in Socks,* and so on.

At a prearranged time on Hat Day, the students can model their hats. The class may take turns guessing the character or Dr. Seuss book depicted. You may want to award prizes for the most original hat, most materials used on a hat, and so on.

On Hat Day, you may want to use the "Dr. Seuss and His Friends" Creative Writing Activity. Each student could write about his or her hat.

A good book to read aloud to the class on Hat Day is Dr. Seuss's *The 500 Hats of Bartholomew Cubbins* (New York: Vanguard Press, 1938).

You may want to videotape the Hat Day events and send the tape home with the students. (Refer to the "Enjoying Language Arts" section at the end of this book.)

"Dr. Seuss and His Friends" Read-at-Home Activity

Encourage the students to read Dr. Seuss books. You will need to determine the number of books you want the students to read and the number of "Dr. Seuss and His Friends" Read-at-Home Activity Pages to send home. If there are a limited number of Dr. Seuss books available, you may prefer to borrow a collection from your school media center. Then circulate the books from your own room with one book at a time going home per child.

"Dr. Seuss and His Friends" Read-at-Home Award

Duplicate the award onto colored paper. Give the award to each child who reads the required number of books and returns the completed "Dr. Seuss and His Friends" Read-at-Home Activity Page.

"Dr. Seuss and His Friends" Spelling Activity

You may want to read aloud the book *Green Eggs and Ham* by Dr. Seuss (New York: Random House, 1960) prior to using this page. Determine the number of pages each student will need for the spelling assignment.

"Dr. Seuss and His Friends" Creative Writing Activity

1. You will need to make a big hat outline on paper. You might want to enlarge the Creative Writing Activity Page's hat.

2. Conduct a class discussion about hats. Write the words the students suggest on the hat. Encourage the students to think of many unique and varied kinds of hats such as bonnet, helmet, stocking, baseball, and so on. Discuss the kinds of materials used to make hats, for example, yarn, straw, felt, cloth. Also talk about what you could find on a hat, for example, feathers, buttons, ribbon, rain, snow, bows, flowers, emblems.

3. Following the hat discussion, each student may cut out the hat on the page, then he or she draws a unique hat on the back of the page. Encourage the student to write about his or her hat on the front side of the page using the hat vocabulary list as a reference. You may want to assemble the hat pages into a class book. The students may contribute more than one page.

"Dr. Seuss and His Friends" Research Activity

1. Duplicate the "un-dictionary" directions for each student. Stress the importance of using words from Dr. Seuss books that cannot be found in a real dictionary. Also emphasize arranging the words in alphabetical order.

2. Determine the number of words you want for this activity, then duplicate the appropriate number of Research Activity Pages.

3. You may prefer to have younger students complete this activity at home with parental help. The child could write the word of his or her choice and dictate a definition to a parent to write down. Then the child could copy the definition onto the page. He or she could illustrate each word.

4. Older students could complete the research activity independently either at home or at school.

5. Arrange a time for the students to share their un-dictionaries. You may want to encourage the students to put them in a reading area of your room. The students may want to share their un-dictionaries with another class, too, as described in "Enjoying Language Arts" at the end of this book.

"Dr. Seuss and His Friends" Student Summary Page

Duplicate the Summary Page for older students to complete independently. You may want to discuss the questions with younger students and help them record their answers on this page. You may wish to graph the summary results.

Hat Day

Date _____

Dear Parent,

As a culminating activity for our Dr. Seuss language arts unit, we will have a Hat Day
on _____ .
Your child will need to make a hat depicting a character or some aspect of a Dr. Seuss
book. The hat may be made out of scrap materials such as paper bags, paper plates,
construction paper, wallpaper, material scraps, beads, feathers, ribbons, and so on. Your
child may prefer to decorate an old hat of his or her own. You may have a family member's
hat which would be suitable for this project.

Please encourage your child to read the Dr. Seuss book of his or her choice and discuss
it with you. Your child should decide the kind of hat that would best represent the book or
one of its characters. He or she should create a unique hat independently from the materials
you have available in your home.

On Hat Day _____ please send the hat in a bag or box with
your child's name on it.

You are welcome to come at _____ on Hat Day _____ to
join the fun! The students will model their hats. The class will take turns guessing the Dr.
Seuss characters and books being depicted.

Thank you for your continued support.

Sincerely,

_____
Your child's teacher

63

"Dr. Seuss and His Friends"
Read-at-Home Activity Page

Return by _____

Date _____

Dear Parent,

During the next two weeks, our language arts learning centers will feature Dr. Seuss books.

Encourage your child to read _____ books written by Dr. Seuss, Theo. Le Sieg, or Theodor Geisel. (Mr. Geisel writes books under the pen names of Dr. Seuss and Theo. Le Sieg.)

Each child who reads the required number of books and completes the attached "Dr. Seuss and His Friends" Read-at-Home Activity Page will receive an award. Please return on _____.

You may enjoy reading some of the books aloud with your child. Perhaps you can share rhymes or tongue twisters that you like with your child.

Thank you for your help with this activity.

Sincerely,

_____
Your child's teacher

"Dr. Seuss and His Friends"
Read-at-Home Activity Page

Return by _____

Reader's Name: _____

Title of book: _____

Author: _____ Illustrator: _____

Date Begun: _____ Date Finished: _____

Parent's Signature: _____

_____

Reader's Name: _____

Title of Book: _____

Author: _____ Illustrator: _____

Date Begun: _____ Date Finished: _____

Parent's Signature: _____

_____

Reader's Name: _____

Title of Book: _____

Author: _____ Illustrator: _____

Date Begun: _____ Date Finished: _____

Parent's Signature: _____

HURRAH for

_____

who read ___ books

by Dr. Seuss.

_____
teacher

Read At Home

BOOM!

POW!

HUR R.A.H!
Read At Home

"Dr. Seuss and His Friends"
Read-at-Home Award

name _____

Write your spelling words
on Sam-I-Am's egg yolks.

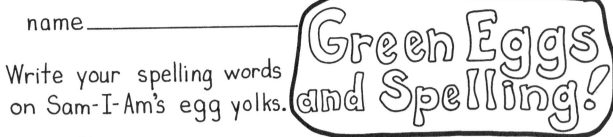
Green Eggs and Spelling!

Color the rest of each egg green.

★ Draw yourself at your favorite place to eat green eggs
and ham on the back of this page.

"Dr. Seuss and His Friends"
Spelling Activity

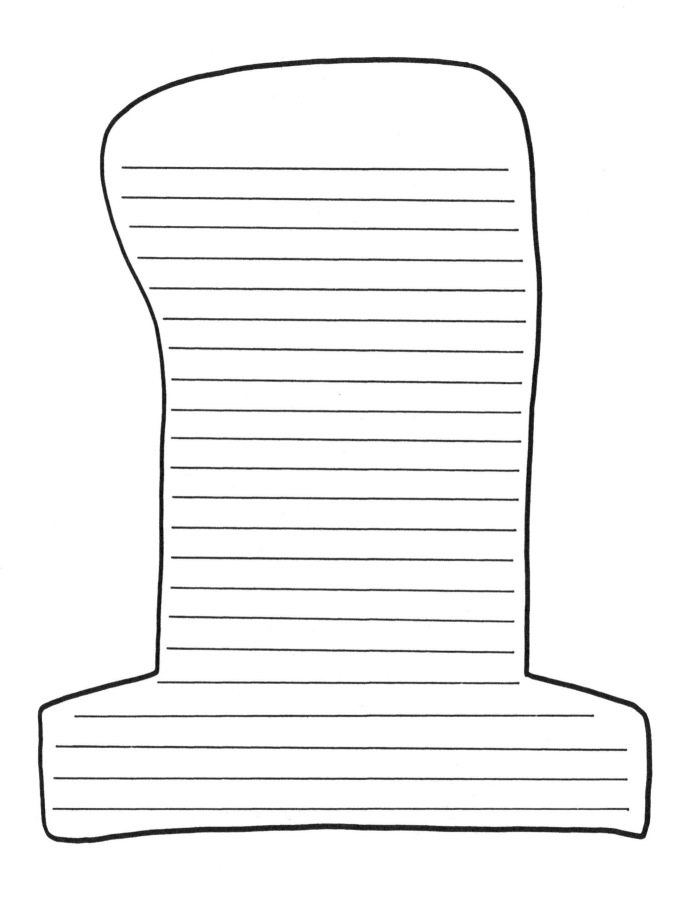

"Dr. Seuss and His Friends"
Creative Writing Activity

Un-dictionary

1. Create an un-dictionary using as many books by Dr. Seuss (Theo. Le Sieg, Theodor Geisel) as you would like.

2. You must find _____ words that cannot be found in a real dictionary. (Look up each one to be sure.)

3. Use one of the attached pages for each word.

4. Write the word and make up a definition describing the word.

5. Illustrate the word in the box.

6. Write the title and the author of the book that you used.

7. Put the pages in alphabetical order.

8. Number each page.

9. Make a cover for your un-dictionary with your name on it.

10. Put your un-dictionary together (staple, use rings, tie with yarn, and so on).

11. Bring your un-dictionary to school on _____ .

"Dr. Seuss and His Friends"
Research Activity

word _____

definition _____

_____

_____

illustration

This word was found in
the book _____
by _____

Un-dictionary page___

Name: _____ Date: _____

"Dr. Seuss and His Friends"
Summary Page

1. My favorite center(s): _____
_____
_____

Why? _____
_____
_____

2. The center(s) I did not like: _____
_____
_____

Why? _____
_____
_____

3. Which Dr. Seuss character would you like to bring home for a pet? _____
Why? _____
_____
_____

How would you keep and feed it? _____
_____
_____
_____

What would your parents say about your pet? _____
_____
_____

4. You may draw a picture about the Dr. Seuss character you chose on the back of this page.

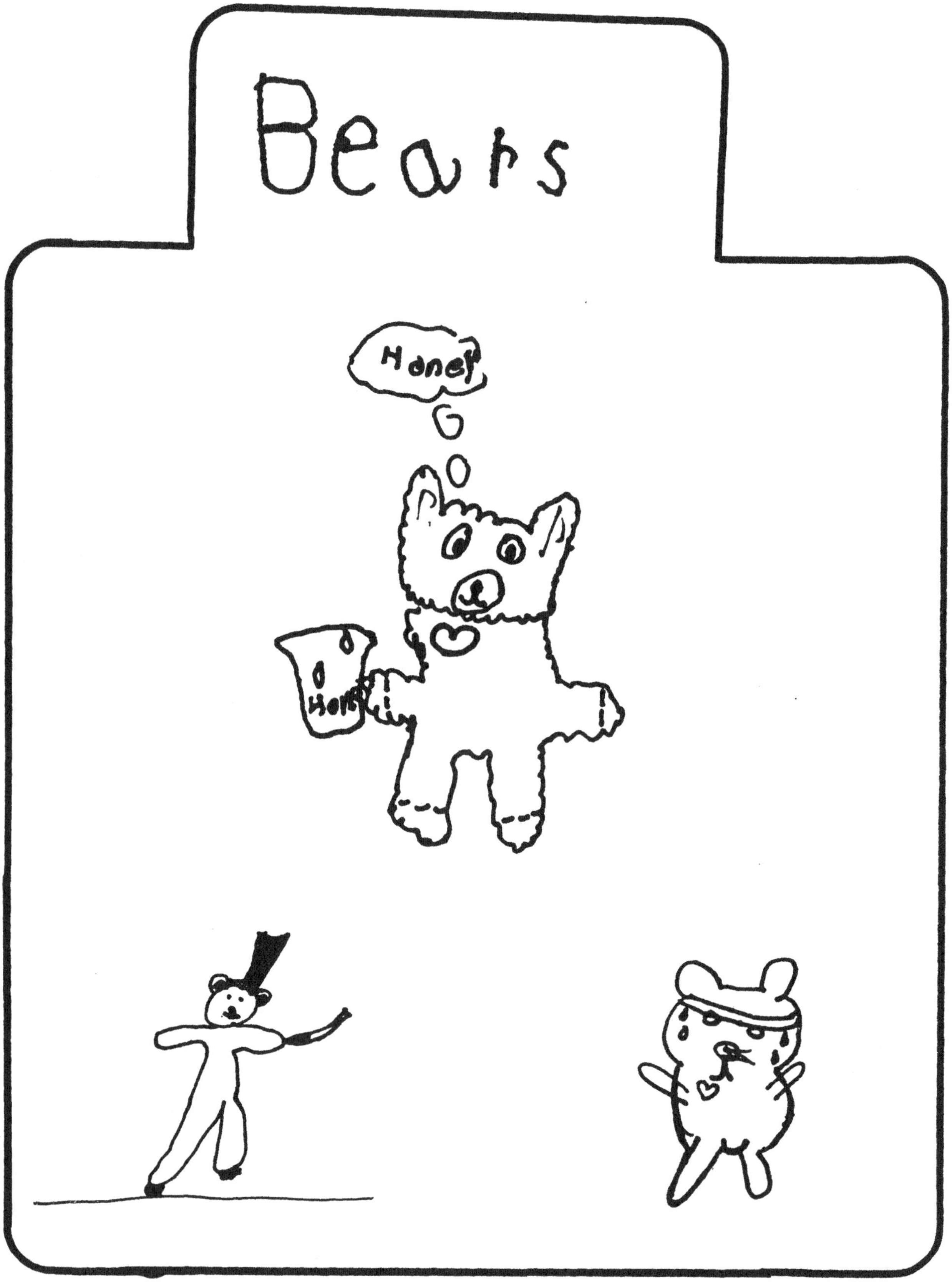
Bears
Honey

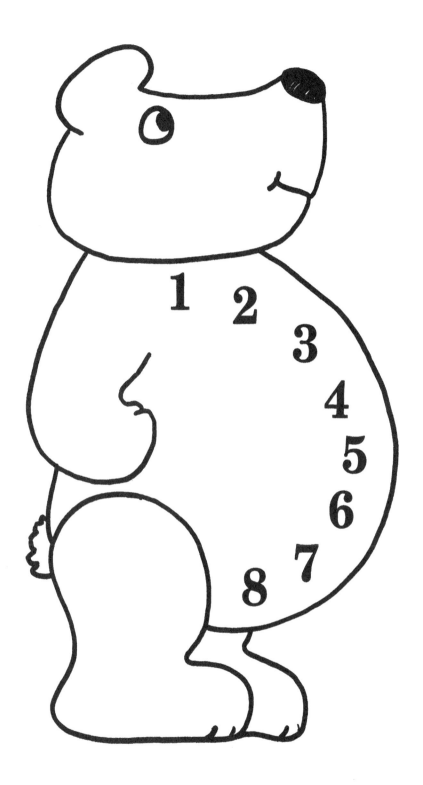

"Bears"
Center Marker

Bears, Bears, Everywhere!

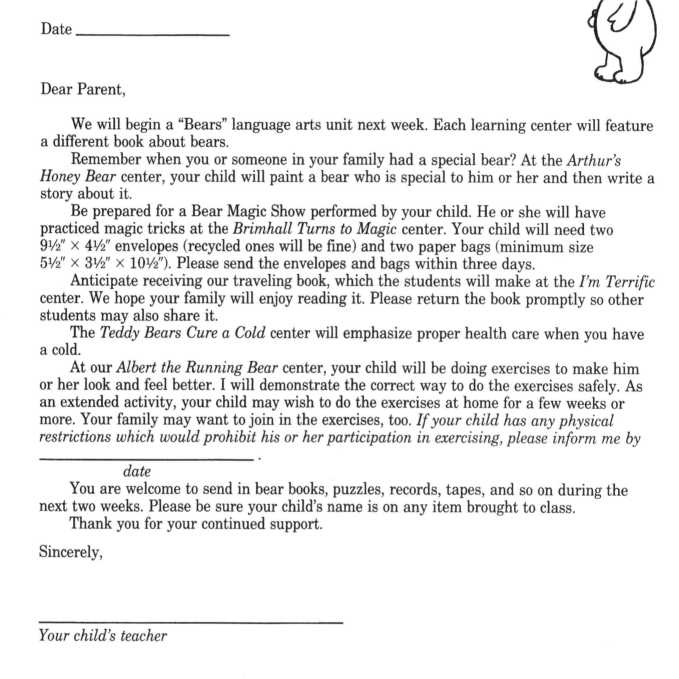

Date _____

Dear Parent,

We will begin a "Bears" language arts unit next week. Each learning center will feature a different book about bears.

Remember when you or someone in your family had a special bear? At the *Arthur's Honey Bear* center, your child will paint a bear who is special to him or her and then write a story about it.

Be prepared for a Bear Magic Show performed by your child. He or she will have practiced magic tricks at the *Brimhall Turns to Magic* center. Your child will need two 9½″ × 4½″ envelopes (recycled ones will be fine) and two paper bags (minimum size 5½″ × 3½″ × 10½″). Please send the envelopes and bags within three days.

Anticipate receiving our traveling book, which the students will make at the *I'm Terrific* center. We hope your family will enjoy reading it. Please return the book promptly so other students may also share it.

The *Teddy Bears Cure a Cold* center will emphasize proper health care when you have a cold.

At our *Albert the Running Bear* center, your child will be doing exercises to make him or her look and feel better. I will demonstrate the correct way to do the exercises safely. As an extended activity, your child may wish to do the exercises at home for a few weeks or more. Your family may want to join in the exercises, too. *If your child has any physical restrictions which would prohibit his or her participation in exercising, please inform me by*

_____ .
      date

You are welcome to send in bear books, puzzles, records, tapes, and so on during the next two weeks. Please be sure your child's name is on any item brought to class.

Thank you for your continued support.

Sincerely,

_____
Your child's teacher

HOTLINE FROM

Parent ——————— TO ——————— School

Date _____

Dear Parent,

    I would appreciate any feedback you or your child may have regarding the "Bears" learning centers: *Jesse Bear, What Will You Wear?*; *Corduroy*; *I'm Terrific*; *Teddy Bears Cure a Cold*; *Little Bear*; *Albert the Running Bear's Exercise Book*; *Arthur's Honey Bear*; and *Brimhall Turns to Magic*.

    Please use this page for comments and return it to me by _____.

Sincerely,

_____

Your child's teacher

Date _____

Dear _____ ,

"BEARS" LEARNING CENTERS LIST

These learning centers feature books about bears.

Jesse Bear, What Will You Wear? Center

(A bulletin board is used with this center)

Skills Reading, using reference materials, fine-motor coordination

Activities

1. Clothespin objects and matching word cards onto the clothesline on the bulletin board.
2. Complete object-word work on the Student Activity Page.

Corduroy Center

Skills Reading, computer, creating, art, fine-motor coordination

Activities

1. Read the book.
2. Use the computer and printer to make a poster.

I'm Terrific Center

Skills Reading, listening, creative writing, fine-motor coordination

Activities

1. Listen to the cassette tape of the book.
2. Complete the work on the Student Activity Pages for a class book.

Albert the Running Bear's Exercise Book Center

Skills Reading, health, fine-motor coordination

Activities

1. Make a sweatband.
2. Do the exercises.

Teddy Bears Cure a Cold Center

Skills Reading, creative writing, fine-motor coordination, art

Activities

1. Make a poster using the Bear Student Activity Page.
2. Write a poem on the Beary Soft Tissue Box Activity Page.

Brimhall Turns to Magic Center

Skills Reading, speaking, creating, fine-motor coordination

Activities

1. Make the bear on the student activity page.
2. Practice the magic tricks in front of the mirror.

Arthur's Honey Bear Center

Skills Reading, creative writing, fine-motor coordination, art, using reference materials

Activities

1. Paint a bear which is special to you.
2. Write a story about your special bear on the student activity page.

Little Bear Center (Open-Ended Activity)

Skills Reading, math, fine-motor coordination, teacher's choice

Activities

1. Sort and count the bears and color the graph.
2. Make number sentences with handfuls of bears.

"BEARS" CENTER MARKER

Distribute copies of the bear marker (refer to page 73) to the students. The students can color, cut out, and place their markers near the "Bears" learning centers.

TEACHER'S DIRECTIONS FOR *JESSE BEAR, WHAT WILL YOU WEAR?* CENTER

Skills Reading, using reference materials, fine-motor coordination

Materials Needed

    Book: Carlstrom, Nancy White, *Jesse Bear, What Will You Wear?*, New York: Macmillan, 1986

    Bulletin board

    Copies of the Student Activity Page (see page 81)

    Teacher-made set of objects and container

    Teacher-made set of object-word cards and container

    Nine clip clothespins and container

    One 6′ piece of clothesline or heavy twine

    Crayons

    Pencil

Materials Preparation

1. Prepare a bulletin board as pictured on the File Folder Directions Page.

2. For the set of objects, you may enlarge the objects on the Student Activity Page onto heavy paper. Laminate the cards and provide a container, such as a clothes basket, for them.

3. To make the set of object-word cards, write the name of the objects on 3″ × 5″ index cards. The objects on the Student Activity Page are rose, shirt, pear, sand, boat, blanket, sun, pants, stars. You may also want to write the words on the back of the objects to make the activity self-checking.

Directions for File Folder Activities

Activity 1

The student clothespins the objects and matching word cards onto the clothesline on the bulletin board.

Activity 2

The student writes the word for each object on the Student Activity Page, referring to the object-word cards, and colors the objects.

Options for older students:

a. Write rhyming words for each object using the book or dictionary as a reference.

b. Fold writing paper in half or thirds and list objects from the book into categories such as clothes, food, and so on.

Takeoff

1. Read aloud the book *Brown Bear, Brown Bear What Do You See?* by Bill Martin, Jr. (New York: Holt, Rhinehart, and Winston, 1970). Then make a pattern class book such as " _____ Bear, _____ Bear What Will You Wear? I'll Wear A _____ _____ Everywhere!"

2. Discuss with the entire class ways they get dressed for school. Graph the ways they get dressed, such as:
   a. Do you pick out your own clothes? (Yes or no)
   b. When do you decide what you will wear? (Night before or morning)
   c. Who decides what you will wear? (You, Mom, Dad, babysitter)

3. Creative writing activity. Suggest topics, such as:
   a. "The funniest thing that happened to me when I was getting dressed . . ."
   b. "The strangest outfit I ever wore . . ."
   c. "On Saturday, I like to wear . . ."
   d. "The outfit I would like to wear to school, but my Mom won't let me . . ."

Jesse Bear, What Will You Wear?

by Nancy White Carlstrom

1

Pin the objects and matching cards on the line.

2

Write the words on the lines.

Jesse Bear, What Will You Wear?
File Folder Directions

name _____

Draw a picture of Jesse Bear wearing what
you liked best on the back.

TEACHER'S DIRECTIONS FOR *CORDUROY* CENTER

Skills Reading, computer, creating, art, fine-motor coordination

Materials Needed

   Book: Freeman, Don, *Corduroy,* New York: Viking Press, 1968
   Computer and printer
   Paper

Materials Preparation

   1. Use a computer and printer with an appropriate print program to create a poster, sign, or banner. If a computer and printer are unavailable, use a medium of your choice for the poster.

   2. As an optional activity, you may want to make a Corduroy sewing card for the student to use at this center as pictured:

Laminate the card, then punch holes in it with a paper puncher. Provide a needle and thread or thin shoelace, and a button for the students to sew onto the card.

Directions for File Folder Activities

   Activity 1

   The student reads the book.

   Activity 2

   The student makes a poster to help find Corduroy's lost button.

Takeoff

1. Read aloud the book to the whole class. Give each child a button to take home. Encourage the students to retell the story at home.

2. Conduct a Button Treasure Hunt in your classroom. Hide buttons in your room. Provide written clues for the students to use in the hunt. The students could play this game in pairs or small groups.

3. You may also want to read the book *A Pocket for Corduroy,* by Don Freeman (New York: Viking Press, 1978).

 # Corduroy

by Don Freeman

1 Read the book.

2 Make a poster to help find Corduroy's lost button.

Corduroy
File Folder Directions

TEACHER'S DIRECTIONS FOR *I'M TERRIFIC* CENTER

Skills Reading, listening, creative writing, fine-motor coordination

Materials Needed

Book: Sharmat, Marjorie Weinman, *I'm Terrific,* New York: Holiday House, 1977

Copies of the Student Activity Page (see page 88)

Teacher-made book

Tape recorder

Cassette tape

Pencil

Crayons

Three gummed gold stars per student and teacher

Materials Preparation

1. Prepare a cassette tape of the book.

2. Make a book by compiling a Student Activity Page for each class member (including yourself) as pictured:

You will begin the book by writing your name on the first page. Demonstrate how to put three gold stars on the forehead of your bear prior to coloring. The next person who participates in the center after you will complete *your* page by giving at least one reason why you deserve three stars on your bear's forehead, coloring the bear, and signing his or her name. Then he or she will prepare the following page by writing his or her name at the top of the page and putting three gold stars on the bear's forehead. Each successive student who uses the center will continue the book in a chain manner. The last page will be completed by you on the final day of the "Bear" centers. The book may become part of a traveling book collection, as described in the last section of this book.

3. *Option for younger students.* Remove the lines on the student activity page prior to duplicating the pages for a book. The student will draw a picture showing a classmate's terrific behavior on a page and color the bear. Then the student may dictate a sentence for a teacher or aide to write the under the picture.

Directions for File Folder Activities

Activity 1

The student listens to the cassette tape of the book.

Activity 2

The student makes the pages for the book per your directions.

Takeoff

1. Students may want additional copies of the Student Activity Page to make a book for a family member or an appreciation book for the support staff at your school. The book can then be shared with support staff using the In-School Note described in the last section of this book.

2. Discuss Jason's behavior in the book with the entire class. You may wish to list the behavior on a chart. Emphasize the fact that Jason recognized a behavior which he decided to change. Ask your students to reflect on their own behaviors and choose one they think they could work on to change. Then ask each student to write or draw a picture of one behavior he or she believes could be changed. Each student will put his or her resolution inside an envelope, seal it, and write his or her name on it. Place all the envelopes in a container such as a shoe box covered with construction paper and decorated with gummed gold stars. After one week, open the container and distribute the envelopes to the students. Each student can look at his or her resolution and decide whether the change in behavior is a one-, two-, or three-star improvement. The appropriate number of stars may be selected and put on the envelope or resolution by the student. The students may take the resolutions and envelopes home to share with their families.

I'm Terrific

by Marjorie Weinman Sharmat

1 Listen to the book.

2 Make the pages for the book.

I'm Terrific
File Folder Directions

_____ is a terrific three-star person because _____

_____

_____

_____

_____

_____

by _____

TEACHER'S DIRECTIONS FOR *ALBERT THE RUNNING BEAR'S EXERCISE BOOK* CENTER

Skills Reading, health, fine-motor coordination

Materials Needed

Book: Isenberg, Barbara, and Marjorie Jaffe, *Albert the Running Bear's Exercise Book,* New York: Clarion Books, 1984

Copies of the Student Activity Page (see page 92)

One 30″ × 2″ strip of fabric per student

Scissors

Crayons

Glue

Stapler and staples

Carpet, mat, or towel

Materials Preparation

1. You may wish to make an example sweatband with the pictures from the File Folder Directions Page attached to the fabric with glue or staples in the correct sequence.

2. Be sure that you are aware of any physical restrictions of your students before you let them participate in the exercises at this center. Demonstrate the exercises for the entire class, stressing the safe and proper way to do them. You may want to have the class practice the exercises with you prior to beginning the center. Provide carpet, mats, or towels for this activity. Determine the required number of exercises.

3. The student may cut out the calendar strip on the student activity page, take it home, and record daily workouts providing he or she does not have any physical restrictions. (Returning the calendar is optional.)

Directions for File Folder Activities

Activity 1

The student makes a sweatband per your example.

Activity 2

The student does the exercises per your directions.

Takeoff

1. Discuss with your class the exercises the whole group could practice for one week at school. You may wish to coordinate this activity with your physical education program. Emphasize the rules for safe exercising which are given in the book. Stress the proper sequence for the exercise activities.

2. You may want to invite an athlete from your high school or community to visit the class. Encourage the athlete to share his or her experience on the importance of exercising to be physically fit.

3. You may also want to read the following books: *Bear and Duck on the Run* by Judy Delton (Niles, IL: Albert Whitman and Co., 1984), and *Albert the Running Bear Gets the Jitters* by Barbara Isenberg and Susan Wolf (New York: Clarion Books, 1987).

Albert the Running Bear's Exercise Book

by Barbara Isenberg and Marjorie Jaffe

① Make your sweatband.

② Now do the exercises.

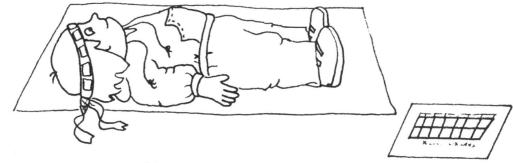

Can you do the exercises at home too?

Albert the Running Bear's Exercise Book
File Folder Directions

Knee Bumps

Wing Circles and Flings

Sun.	Mon.	Tues.	Wed	Thur.	Fri.	Sat.

Put an X if you eXercise!

TEACHER'S DIRECTIONS FOR *TEDDY BEARS CURE A COLD* CENTER

Skills Reading, creative writing, fine-motor coordination, art

Materials Needed

Book: Gretz, Susanna, and Alison Sage, *Teddy Bears Cure a Cold,* New York: Scholastic, 1984

Copies of Student Activity Pages (see pages 96 and 97)

One sheet of 4½″ × 6″ brown construction paper per student

One tissue per student

Scissors

Crayons

Pencil

Glue

Teacher-made example of poem

Materials Preparation

Write a poem about sneezing. Here is an example by Nancy Van Matre:

"Tissue, Please!"
When you're sick
And need to sneeze,
Catch those germs
With a tissue—PLEASE!

Directions for File Folder Activities

Activity 1

The student colors the Bear Student Activity Page 1 (the bear's nose should be colored red). The student glues a tissue at the bottom of the bear's nose. He or she traces his or her hand on brown construction paper to create a paw. Then the student cuts out the paw and glues it over the tissue.

Activity 2

The student writes an original poem or copies your example on the Beary Soft Tissue Box Student Activity Page 2. He or she may color the tissue and the box.

Takeoff

1. Make a class graph featuring things that the students do when they are home sick.

2. Interview a local physician regarding colds (prevention, remedies, and so on). Give the students the opportunity to ask questions.

3. Discuss ways to be healthy, such as eating nutritious foods from the four food groups, washing germs off of hands, getting an adequate amount of sleep, and so on. Let the students take turns giving "Public Service Health Tips from Room _____ " on your school's public address system.

4. Make "Get Well" cards for someone who is sick.

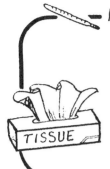

AHH-CHOOO! • SNIFF-SNUFF • KER-CHOO!

Teddy Bears Cure a Cold

by Susanna Gretz and Alison Sage

① Make your poster.

② Write the poem.

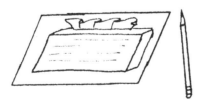

Teddy Bears Cure a Cold
File Folder Directions

When you sneeze, Cover it please!

name _____

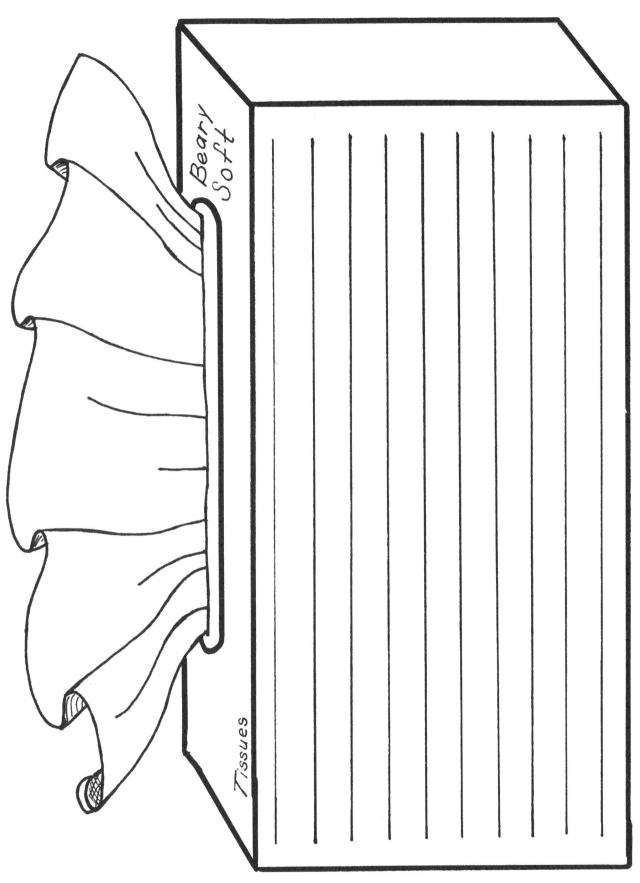

Beary Soft

Tissues

Teddy Bears Cure a Cold
Student Activity Page 2

TEACHER'S DIRECTIONS FOR *BRIMHALL TURNS TO MAGIC* CENTER

Skills Reading, speaking, creating, fine-motor coordination

Materials Needed

Book: Delton, Judy, *Brimhall Turns to Magic,* New York: William Morrow and Co., 1979

Copies of the Student Activity Page (see page 101)

Teacher-made example of bear

Two 9½″ × 4½″ envelopes per student

Spool of white thread

Two paper bags per student (approximately 5½″ × 3½″ × 10½″)

Masking tape

Rubber or plastic comb

Mirror

Scissors

Crayons

Optional: Magic wand (paint a pencil black and add white tape for a stripe; cape (dark piece of fabric); hat

Materials Preparation

1. Make an example of the bear on the Student Activity Page. Attach the thread onto the back of the bear's head with masking tape as shown on the File Folder Directions Page.

2. Demonstrate the tricks:

   a. *Bear in an empty bag trick.* Put one bag inside another bag. Slip the bear between the inside bag and the outside bag. Show the class the empty inside bag. Say the magic words of your choice and pull out the bear. You may also wish to put the comb, scissors, and envelope between the bags and pull them out one at a time.

   b. *Magic moving hair trick.* Prior to demonstrating this trick, tape the tines on one side of a comb. Encourage the student to rub the comb on his or her clothing (not through his or her hair for sanitary reasons). Emphasize wearing a dark-colored shirt in contrast to the white thread "hair." To perform the trick, rub the comb against your clothing. Say some magic words. Wave the comb above the bear's head (the hair will move because it will be attracted to the comb).

   c. *Cut a bear in half trick.* Show the students how to prepare the bear and the envelope for the trick, referring to the Student Activity Page. Then slip the bear into the envelope slits. Cut the bear in half. Say some magic words and pull out the bear. (Emphasize cutting the envelope only, not the bear!) Note the student will have two envelopes to use, one to practice the trick at school and another to perform the trick at home.

3. Share hints with the students for performing a good magic trick:
   a. Practice in front of a mirror to see how you look.
   b. Talk while you are doing a trick.
   c. Don't tell your audience what you are really going to do, only what you want them to *think* you are doing. *Never* tell the secret of performing the trick.

4. Optional: If you wish to have the students perform additional tricks, refer to the *Brimhall Turns to Magic* book. Additional sources are: *More Magic Tricks* by Judith Conway (Mahwah, NJ: Troll Associates, 1987); *Funny Magic* by Rose Wyler and Gerald Ames (New York: Parents' Magazine Press, 1972); *Magic Secrets* by Rose Wyler and Gerald Ames (New York: Bantam Doubleday Dell, 1990).

Directions for File Folder Activities

Activity 1

The student colors and cuts out the bear on the Student Activity Page.

Activity 2

The student prepares the bear and practices the tricks in front of the mirror per your directions.

Optional: The student may write his or her name (" _____ 's Magic Bag") on the outside of the bag and decorate it by coloring it with crayons.

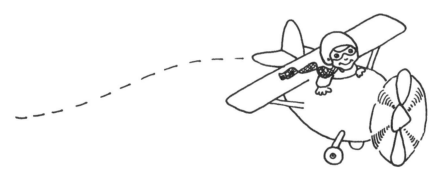

Takeoff

1. Videotape your student magicians. Send the tape home on a rotating basis. (See the last section of this book for details.)

2. Arrange for the students to perform a magic show for parents, another class (see the last section of this book), a hospital, a nursing home, or a senior citizens' group.

3. Make a traveling magic show. Assemble several tricks in a bag. The students can take turns sending the bag home, similar to the traveling books described in the last section of this book.

Brimhall Turns to Magic
by Judy Delton

1. Make your magic bear.

(back)

Tape the "hair" on the back of it's head.

2. Practice the tricks in front of the mirror. Practice what you will say!

① Bear in an empty bag trick.

② Magic moving hair trick

③

Brimhall Turns to Magic
File Folder Directions

Cut a Bear in Half !

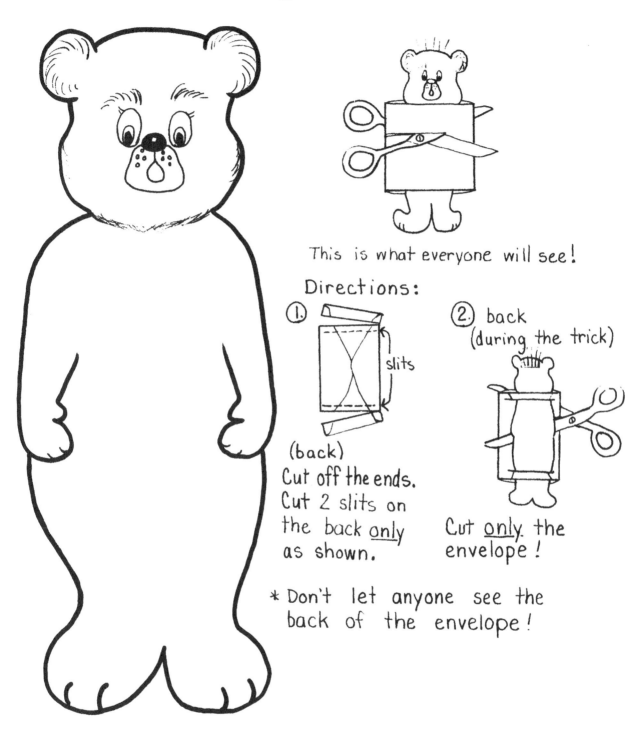

This is what everyone will see!

Directions:

① (back)
Cut off the ends.
Cut 2 slits on the back only as shown.

slits

② back (during the trick)

Cut only the envelope !

* Don't let anyone see the back of the envelope !

TEACHER'S DIRECTIONS FOR *ARTHUR'S HONEY BEAR* CENTER

Skills Reading, creative writing, fine-motor coordination, art, using reference materials

Materials Needed

Book: Hoban, Lillian, *Arthur's Honey Bear,* New York: Harper and Row, 1974
Copies of the Student Activity Page (see page 105)
Easel
Paint
Paintbrushes
Old shirt
Paper
Pencil
Crayons
References (pictionary, dictionary)

Materials Preparation

You may wish to read or display other security bear books at this center, such as Martha Alexander's *We're in Trouble Blackboard Bear* (New York: Dial Press, 1980) and Bernard Waber's *Ira Sleeps Over* (Boston: Houghton-Mifflin, 1972).

Directions for File Folder Activities

Activity 1

The student paints a bear which is special to him or her.

Activity 2

The student writes a story about his or her special bear on the Student Activity Page.

Takeoff

1. The students could have a tag sale in the classroom. Divide the class into small groups: Group 1 students could price and label items in your room such as books, games, pencils, paste, scissors, crayons, tape, paper, and so on. Group 2 students could set up a display area for the items and make signs. Group 3 students could use coin stamps, stamp pads, and paper to make money. (Optional: Cut out money from math book pages or appropriate money duplicating Masters.) The students in the three groups could take turns being salespeople.

Each student could have a prearranged amount of play money to spend on the items. He or she could make a wish list or draw pictures of the items to be purchased. Then the student could shop for the items, write the prices on the list, make appropriate choices, and total the amount of money spent.

2. The students may wish to do a research project regarding the origin of teddy bears.

Arthur's Honey Bear
by Lillian Hoban

1  Paint a picture of a bear that is special to you.

2 Now write about your bear.

Arthur's Honey Bear
File Folder Directions

name

Arthur's Honey Bear
Student Activity Page

TEACHER'S DIRECTIONS FOR *LITTLE BEAR* CENTER

Skills Reading, math, fine-motor coordination, teacher's choice

Materials Needed

　　Book: Minarik, Else Holmelund, *Little Bear,* New York: Harper and Row, 1957

　　Copies of the Student Activity Pages (see pages 109 and 110)

　　Plastic counting bears in red, yellow, green, and blue—no more than ten per color (these are available in most school-product catalogs)

　　Container for bears

　　Four smaller containers labeled "red," "yellow," "green," "blue"

　　Crayons

　　Pencil

Materials Preparation

　　1. Prepare a counting bear container similar to the one pictured on the File Folder Directions. If no plastic teddy bear counters are available, you could dye bear-shaped macaroni in the four colors in the following manner: Shake the macaroni in a container of 8 parts rubbing alcohol to 1 part food coloring, then spread the dyed bears on newspapers to dry.

　　2. Determine the number of colors of counting bears the students will manipulate for number sentences. That number is inserted in the blank on Student Activity Page 2 prior to duplication.

Directions for File Folder Activities

　　Activity 1

　　The student sorts and counts the counting bears into the four labeled, small containers. The information is colored on the graph on Student Activity Page 1.

　　Activity 2

　　The student combines the teacher's prearranged number of bears back into the original container of bears. The student grabs a handful of bears, counts the bears in that handful, and records a number sentence that describes the bears. For example, with three colors of bears in the container, the handful of three yellow, four red, and two blue bears could be written as $3 + 4 + 2 = 9$. A subtraction problem could be created by hiding a random number of bears from the handful in a "cave" container and counting the remaining bears. For example: nine bears in the handful, the student "hides" two under a bowl or in a cupped hand and writes the following number sentence of $9 - 2 = 7$. (The colors of bears can be disregarded in subtraction.) Each number sentence is recorded on Student Activity Page 2.

Takeoff

Counting bears like the ones used in this center may be manipulated for a wide variety of math activities during the period of time your class uses the "Bear" learning centers. Here are just a few activities to use:

1. Students may write word problems for bears, such as: Six bears meet two more bears and go on a picnic. How many bears are there in all? Students may solve each other's word problems.

2. Students may write all possible combinations for a teacher-designated number, such as 7. The students manipulate two colors of bears to find the combinations and record the number sentences on paper.

3. Provide common classroom objects (erasers, books, etc.) and a balance scale. Have the students predict the weight of each object in teddy bear units and then weigh the objects on the balance scale. Compare, contrast, add, and subtract the findings.

4. More or less? Two students may each grab a handful of bears and estimate—without first actually counting—who had more or less. The students then count to determine who had more or less.

Little Bear
by Else Holmelund Minarik

1 Sort and count the little bears. Color the graph.

2 Make number sentences with handfuls of bears.

Little Bear
File Folder Directions

Graphing Bears

Sort and count the bears.　　name_____

	red	yellow	green	blue
10				
9				
8				
7				
6				
5				
4				
3				
2				
1				

Little Bear
Student Activity Page 1

Handfuls of Bears

Make number sentences with the bears. Use ___ colors of bears. Use a different handful for each sentence.

Bears Enrichment Activities

Teddy Bears Picnic

TEACHER'S DIRECTIONS FOR "BEARS" ENRICHMENT ACTIVITIES

"Bears" Group Activity

As a culminating activity to the "Bears" language arts unit, schedule a Teddy Bear Day. The following are activities you may want to do.

1. Plan a Teddy Bears' Picnic:
   a. Ask each student to bring in a stuffed bear. (If not possible, the student can bring in a picture of a bear.)
   b. Have each student bring a lunch for the picnic, or you may prefer to serve a light snack of berries and bear-shaped crackers.
   c. If desired, have the students write invitations to parents to attend the picnic also.
   d. Provide blankets for the people and the bears to use for the picnic.
   e. Some good books to read aloud at the picnic are *The Bear's Picnic* by Stan and Jan Berenstain (New York: Random House, 1966), *The Teddy Bear's Picnic* by Jimmy Kennedy (New York: Bedrick/Blackie, 1987), or *The Bear's Picnic* by John Yeoman (New York: Macmillan, 1970).
   f. Take the students and parents on a Bear Hunt via the book *I'm Going on a Bear Hunt* by Sandra Stroner Sivulich (New York: E. P. Dutton, 1973).

2. Alternative stuffed-bear activities if you prefer not to have a picnic:
   a. Encourage each student to bring a stuffed bear and a book that his or her bear may enjoy listening to. Arrange a quiet time during the day for the students to read to their bears.
   b. Make "My Favorite Bear" books. Some ideas to include are age and color of the bear, name of the person who gave the bear to the student, the bear's favorite "stuffed" playmate, the bear's worst enemy, the bear's favorite food, why the bear is special, and so on.
   c. Take a photograph of each student with his or her bear. Send it home later or include it in the "My Favorite Bear" books.
   d. Measure the stuffed bears. Graph the kinds, colors, and sizes of bears.

3. Estimate the number of small bear cookies in a large transparent jar. Then count the cookies. The child who guesses the closest gets to distribute the cookies to the class.

4. Tell bear jokes and riddles. A good source is *Grin and Bear It, The Teddy Bear Joke Book* by Suzanne Lord (New York: Parachute Press, 1986). The students may want to write and share their own bear jokes and riddles, too. These could be compiled into a class book to be shared with families.

5. As a spinoff to *Albert the Running Bear's Exercise Book,* let the students jump rope. They may want to make up jingles to chant as they jump.

6. Videotape the Teddy Bear Day activities and send the tape home with the students. (See the last section of this book for details.)

"Bears" Read-at-Home Activity

Read aloud the following books to the class: *Too Much TV* by Stan and Jan Berenstain (New York: Random House, 1984) and *Fix-It* by David McPhail (New York: E. P. Dutton, 1984). Discuss alternatives to television watching.

Declare a specific T.N.T. (Today No Television) day. About one week prior to T.N.T. day, send home the parent letter. Encourage the students to read one book on T.N.T. and return the "Bears" Read-at-Home Activity Page. As a class project, the students could make T.N.T. signs to put on their television sets one day prior to T.N.T.

"Bears" Read-at-Home Award

Duplicate the award onto colored paper. Give the award to each child who fulfills the requirements and returns the completed "Bears" Read-at-Home Activity Page.

"Bears" Spelling Activity

You may want to read aloud the book *Blueberries for Sal* by Robert McCloskey (New York: Viking Press, 1948) prior to using these pages. Determine the number of first-part pages each student will need for the spelling assignment.

The student writes his or her spelling words on the blueberries and cuts them out. Then the student writes the words on the pail envelope on page 2 of the activity. The student colors, cuts out, and staples the pail as per the directions on page 2. The student then places the blueberries from the first page into the pail.

"Bears" Creative-Writing Activity

Read aloud the following books to the class: *The Bike Lesson* by Stan and Jan Berenstain (New York: Random House, 1964) and *The Bear's Bicycle* by Emilie Warren McLeod (Boston: Little, Brown, 1975). Discuss the bicycle safety rules. Determine the number of safety rules you wish to have each student write on the "Bears" Creative Writing Activity Page. Younger students could each do one page and send home or compile pages into a class book. Older students could do several pages and compile them into individual books.

"Bears" Book Report Activity

Each student reads a story about a bear. He or she then pretends to interview the bear on the Book Report Activity Page. You will need to determine the length of time to complete the book report activity. Younger students could dictate the information to a parent to complete the page. (If you have a Teddy Bear Day, set the deadline for the book report activity page to be returned a few days prior to Teddy Bear Day. (The students may wish to share their interviews on Teddy Bear Day.)

"Bears" Summary Page

You may want to conduct a class discussion to review the bear books that have been read during the past two weeks. Then have each student complete the "Summary" page. Arrange a time for the students to share their elevator experiences that they wrote on the summary.

"Bears" Read-at-Home Activity Page

Return by _____

Date _____

Dear Parent,

The theme of our current language arts learning centers is bears. Many books written by Stan and Jan Berenstain are class favorites. Recently, I read aloud their book *Too Much TV*. In addition, I read David McPhail's book *Fix-It*.

After the books were read, the students held a lively discussion. They suggested a variety of activities (reading, family games, sports, and so on) as alternatives to watching television.

Our class had decided to declare _____ as T.N.T. (Today No Television). We encourage your whole family to participate!

Each student will receive an award if he or she fulfills *all* of the following requirements:

1. Do *not* watch television, play video games, or watch videos at any time during the day of _____ .
2. Read one book.
3. Return the attached "Bears" Read-at-Home Activity Page with a parent's signature by _____ .

You may want to go to the library with your child to choose a book your child may want to read on T.N.T. day. You may also want to select some of your own favorite books to read aloud.

Thank you for your help with this activity.

Sincerely,

_____
Your child's teacher

"Bears" Read-at-Home Activity Page

Return by _____

T.N.T.
(TODAY NO TELEVISION)

_____ did it! He or she did NOT watch television, play
Student's name
video games, or watch videos at any time during the day of _____ .
He or she read the book:

TITLE _____

AUTHOR _____

_____
Parent's signature

Would you like to try another T.N.T. day next
month? _____
Please write any comments about family
activities on T.N.T. day on the back of this
sheet. Thank you.
Remember, this form *must* be returned
by _____

Did it !

He/she went the entire day without watching T.V., movies, or playing video games. **HURR.A.H.** for you!

_____ teacher

START

FINISH!

HURR.A.H.!
Read At Home

"Bears"
Read-at-Home Award

Blueberries for Spelling

Write your words on the blueberries.
Cut them out. Put them in your pail.

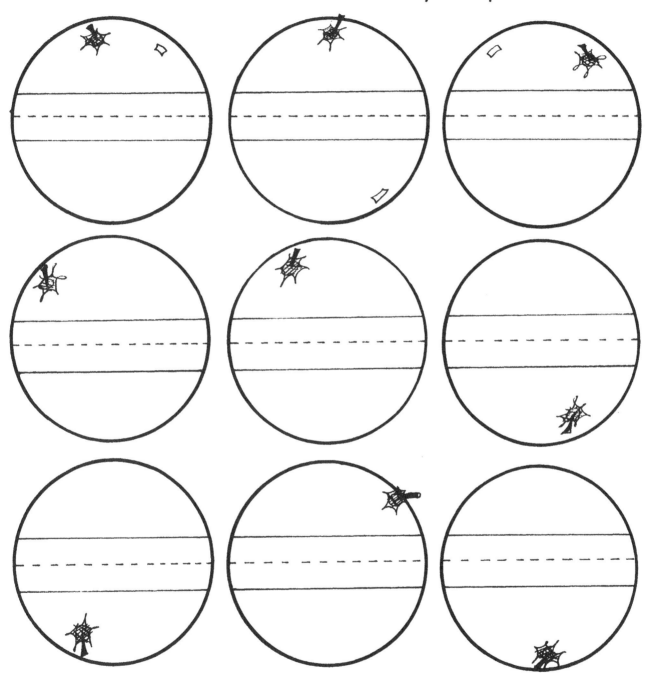

Cut out the pail. Fold on the dashed line.
Staple the side and bottom.

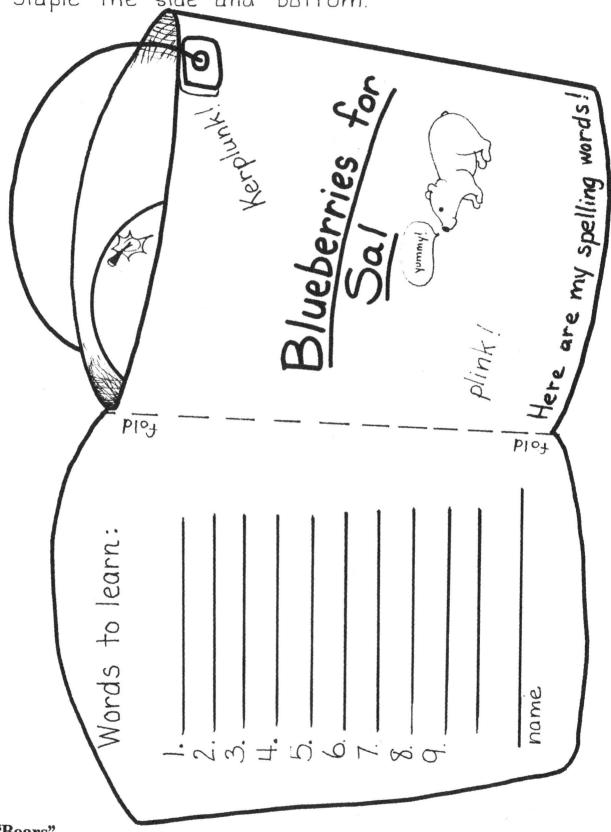

Kerplunk!

Blueberries for Sal

Yummy!

plink!

Here are my spelling words!

fold

fold

Words to learn:

1. _____
2. _____
3. _____
4. _____
5. _____
6. _____
7. _____
8. _____
9. _____

name _____

"Bears"
Spelling Activity Page 2

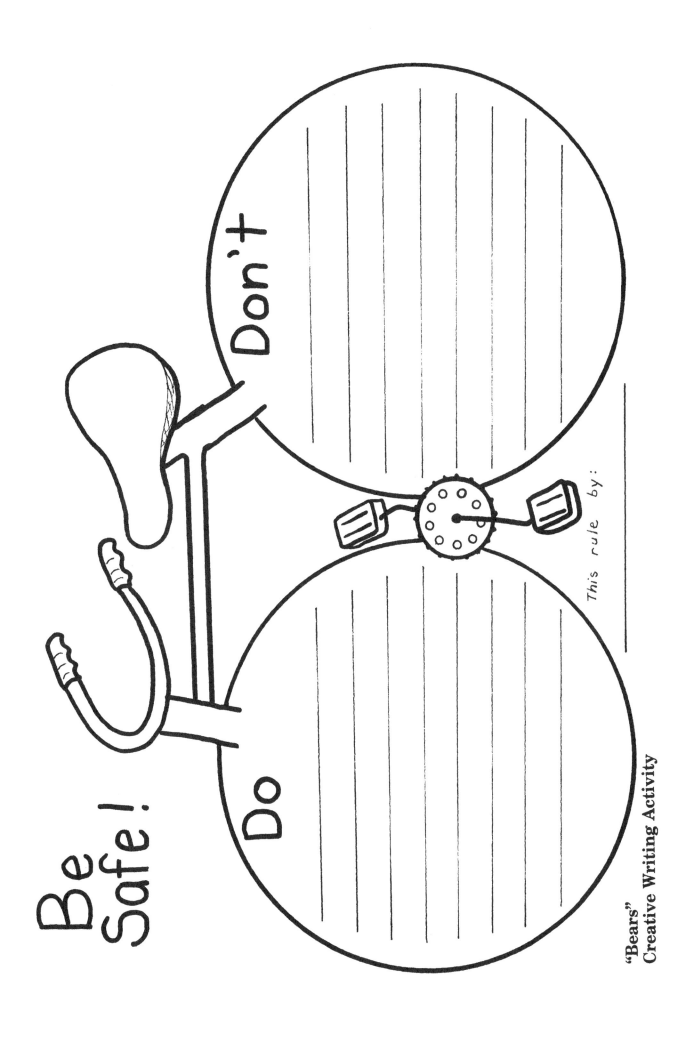

Be Safe!

Don't

Do

This rule by: _____

"Bears"
Creative Writing Activity

Bear Interview

Read a story about a bear. Pretend you are interviewing him or her. Answer these questions as you think the bear in your story might—even if the answer was not in the story!

Bear's name: _____

Book's title: _____

Author's name: _____

Illustrator's name: _____

QUESTIONS FOR THE BEAR

1. In what year were you born? _____

2. Do you have any special animal and/or human friends? _____

   What are their names? _____

   _____

3. Where do you live? _____

4. Why do you think your readers like you? _____

   _____

5. Is there another famous bear you would like to meet? _____

   Who? _____

   Why? _____

6. What is your favorite food? _____

7. What are you afraid of? _____

   When did you first begin to have this fear? _____

   _____

8. What is your favorite T.V. show? _____

9. What are your special hobbies? _____

   _____

INTERVIEWED BY: _____

"Bears"
Book Report Activity Page

Stuck with _____

Of all the bears you have read about, which one would you want to be with on a broken elevator? Why? Write on the lines. Cut the elevator out. Draw the two of you inside the elevator.

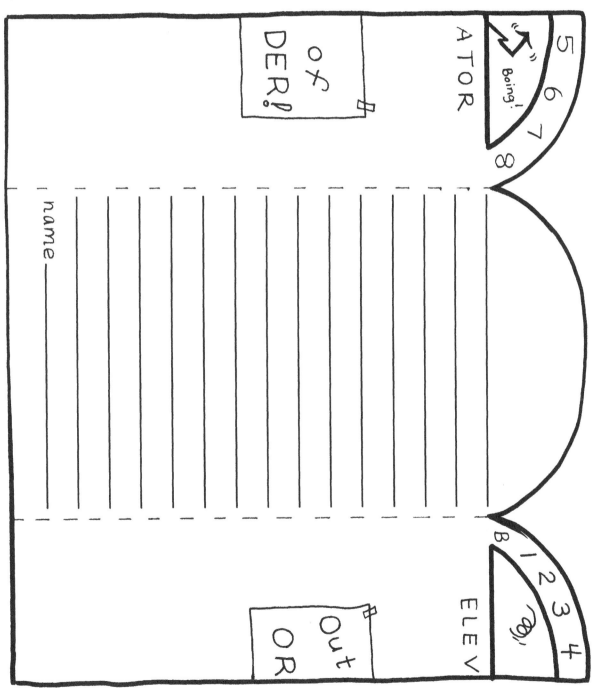

Dogs

snoopy

Pinkerton

Clifford

"Dogs"
Center Marker

Dogs! Dogs! and More Dogs!

Date _____

Dear Parent,

In two weeks we will begin a set of language arts learning centers emphasizing dog books.

One center will feature Snoopy. Our class would appreciate having several "Peanuts" comic strips by Charles M. Schulz from newspapers, recycled books, or wrapping paper. Your child will create his or her own comic strip and view it in the center's Snoopy Show Box. He or she may wish to make additional comic strips and a shoe-box viewer at home.

Anticipate receiving a travel mobile from the *Clifford Takes a Trip* center. Please send any postcards, pamphlets, or souvenirs (with your child's name on them) from the _____ area that you may wish to share for a bulletin board display.

At the computer center, your child will have an opportunity to write a newspaper article that a dog might like to read. The idea is a spinoff from the book *Mrs. Dunphy's Dog*.

Encourage your child to retell the story *Mine Will, Said John* with the props he or she has created. Using a lighted lamp with a white shade will be helpful. At the center, your child will practice with an overhead projector.

A "Changing Box" will be designed by your child at the *Dog for a Day* center. Your child will need a shoe box, facial tissue box or a cereal box. Any junk materials such as cardboard tubes, lids, small boxes, straws, wallpaper, and so on will be welcomed.

Steven Kellogg has written many delightful books about his huge, lovable dog Pinkerton, which your family may enjoy. *Tallyho, Pinkerton!* will be featured at one of our centers.

Please send any of the requested materials within two weeks.

Thank you for your continued support!

Sincerely,

_____

Your child's teacher

HOTLINE FROM

Parent ——————— TO ——————— School

Date _____

Dear Parent,

    I would appreciate any feedback you or your child may have regarding the "Dog" learning centers: *Clifford Takes a Trip; Snoopy; No Roses for Harry; Mrs. Dunphy's Dog; Give a Dog a Bone; Tallyho, Pinkerton!; Dog for a Day;* and *Mine Will, Said John.*
    Please use this page for comments and return it to me by _____ .

Sincerely,

_____

Your child's teacher

Date _____

Dear _____ ,

"DOGS" LEARNING CENTERS LIST

These learning centers feature books about dogs.

Clifford Takes a Trip Center

(a bulletin board is used with this center)

Skills Reading, art, using reference materials, fine-motor coordination

Activities

1. Look for four places on the bulletin board to travel with Clifford.
2. Make a travel mobile about you and Clifford.

Snoopy Center

Skills Reading, art, creative writing, using reference materials, fine-motor coordination

Activities

1. Put the comic stories in order.
2. Make a comic strip about Snoopy. Show it to a friend.

No Roses for Harry Center

Skills Reading, art, fine-motor coordination

Activities

1. Trace the coat pattern and cut it out.
2. Paint Harry in his new coat.

Mrs. Dunphy's Dog Center

Skills Reading, computer, using reference materials, creative writing, fine-motor coordination

Activities

1. Cut out a newspaper article that a dog would like to read. Paste it on paper.
2. Write a newspaper story for a dog.

Mine Will, Said John **Center**

Skills Reading, speaking, creating, fine-motor coordination, science

Activities

    1. Make the animal props for the story.

    2. Practice retelling the story on the overhead projector.

Tallyho, Pinkerton! **Center**

Skills Reading, science, using reference materials, fine-motor coordination

Activities

    1. Look for the mammals and birds in the book.

    2. Help the girl do her homework.

Dog for a Day **Center (Open-Ended Activity)**

Skills Reading, art, math, speaking, fine-motor coordination, teacher's choice

Activities

    1. Make a "changing box."

    2. Make cards that will change in the box.

Give a Dog a Bone **Center**

Skills Reading, listening, speaking, art, creative writing, fine-motor coordination

Activities

    1. Listen to the story.

    2. Make a "Bone" book.

"DOGS" CENTER MARKER

Distribute copies of the dog marker (refer to page 123) to the students. The students can color and cut out their markers, then place them near the "Dogs" learning centers.

TEACHER'S DIRECTIONS FOR *CLIFFORD TAKES A TRIP* CENTER

Skills Reading, art, using reference materials, fine-motor coordination

Materials Needed

    Book: Bridwell, Norman, *Clifford Takes a Trip*, New York: Scholastic, 1966

    Bulletin board

    Pictures, postcards, pamphlets, magazines

    One piece of 32″ × 10″ oaktag or posterboard per student

    Crayons or markers

    Pencil

    Paste or glue

    Paper puncher

    Yarn or wire

    Teacher-made travel mobile

Materials Preparation

1. Determine the geographical area you want your students to visit with Clifford. You may highlight your own state or another state, region, or country. Display on a bulletin board magazine pictures, posters, picture postcards, souvenirs, and so on, from the featured area. Title the board "Clifford Takes a Trip to _____ ."

2. You may include travel magazines, pamphlets, maps, travel posters, and slides with an inexpensive slide viewer at this center. (Travel agencies, automobile clubs, bureaus of tourism, or chambers of commerce are good sources of information.) Encourage the students to bring materials also.

3. Make a travel mobile as pictured on the file folder directions:
   a. Fold a 32″ × 10″ piece of oaktag into four sections. Make a ½″ folded flap at one end of the oaktag.
   b. Draw a picture of yourself with Clifford at four different locations (one per section). You may wish to write one or two descriptive sentences below each picture.
   c. Paste or glue the flap to the opposite end of the oaktag forming a box.
   d. Use a paper puncher to make a hole near the top of each section of the box.
   e. Thread yarn or wire through each hole, tie, and join the ends together to form a hanger for a mobile.
   f. Optional: Younger students may make a 9″ × 12″ oaktag mobile featuring two trip locations (one on each side).

Directions for File Folder Activities

Activity 1

The student reads and examines the materials on the bulletin board. He or she chooses four places to visit with Clifford.

Activity 2

The student makes a travel mobile per your directions.

Takeoff

1. The students may write postcards from their destinations.

2. Discuss the methods of transportation to the areas chosen. Solve these problems: How would Clifford go on a cruise; a ski vacation; to the beach; the farm; a busy, crowded city; and so on.

3. Prepare a passport for Clifford to travel to a foreign country.

Clifford Takes a Trip
by Norman Bridwell

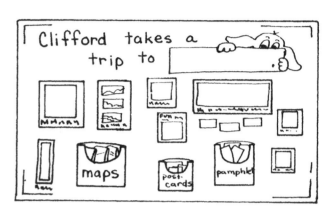

① Look for four places to travel with Clifford.

② Make a travel mobile about Clifford and you.

Clifford Takes a Trip
File Folder Directions

TEACHER'S DIRECTIONS FOR *SNOOPY* CENTER

Skills Reading, art, creative writing, using reference materials, fine-motor coordination

Materials Needed

> A collection of books about Snoopy by Charles M. Schulz, such as *Snoopy* (New York: Holt, Rinehart and Winston, 1958)
>
> A collection of "Peanuts" comics by Charles M. Schulz
>
> Copies of the Student Reference Page (see page 134)
>
> Pencil
>
> Crayons or washable fine-tip marking pens
>
> Adding machine tape or strips of paper
>
> Teacher-made Snoopy Show Box
>
> Teacher-made frame pattern
>
> Teacher-made comic strip

Materials Preparation

1. Provide a collection of "Peanuts" comic strips by Charles M. Schulz which have an obvious sequence of events. Possible sources are newspapers, wrapping paper, recycled books, and so on, which were requested in the parent letter. Cut out the comic-strip pictures and mount them on colored tagboard cards (use a different color of tagboard for each comic story). You may want to number the backs of each set of cards to make the sequencing of the story self-checking. Laminate the cards and provide a container for them. You may wish to use a set of cards to use as a sequencing example.

2. Use a shoe box to make a Snoopy Show Box as pictured on the file folder directions. Cut out a rectangular "window" in one end of the box (approximately 2½″ × 4″). Also cut a 2½″ slit on each side of the box.

3. You determine the size of the paper for the student's comic strips such as 2½″ adding machine tape. Make an oaktag frame pattern slightly smaller than the rectangular "window" of the box. Show the students how to trace the pattern onto the paper to create frames for the comic strip. You may wish to determine a specific number of pictures per strip.

4. Make a comic strip featuring some of the cartooning techniques shown on the Snoopy Student Reference Page. Encourage the students to use the reference page as well as the Snoopy books for cartooning ideas.

5. Demonstrate the proper procedure for threading the comic strip through the slits in the Snoopy Show Box.

Directions for File Folder Activities

Activity 1

The student puts the comic stories in sequential order.

Activity 2

The student makes a comic strip about Snoopy. He or she puts the comic strip into the Snoopy Show Box and shows it to a friend.

Takeoff

1. Divide the class into small groups to make comic strips. The groups can take turns presenting shows with the Snoopy Show Box to the class or other students in your school. (See "Enjoying Language Arts" for more details.)

2. Encourage the students to bring the newspaper comic pages to class. They can compare animal comic strips, cartooning techniques, styles, and so on.

3. Use a computer and Snoopy software.

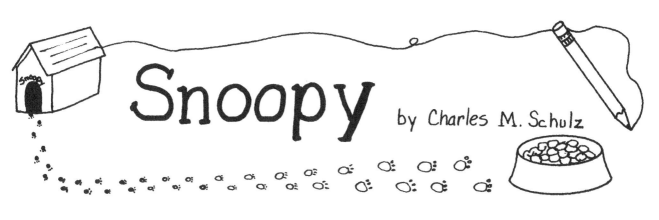

Snoopy

by Charles M. Schulz

1 Put the stories in order.

2 Make a comic strip about Snoopy.

frame pattern

Show it to a friend.

Snoopy
File Folder Directions

Tricks for Cartooning

Here are ways to make your cartoons look like ones in newspapers and books.

Running

Travel lines

Movement

A thought

Sleeping

Love

Angry Words

Bright Idea!

Sound

Wet / Rain

Hands

Sign the last frame.

TEACHER'S DIRECTIONS FOR *NO ROSES FOR HARRY* CENTER

Skills Reading, art, fine-motor coordination

Materials Needed

Book: Zion, Gene, *No Roses for Harry,* New York: Harper and Row, 1958
An assortment of wallpaper, construction paper, wrapping paper
Paint
Paintbrushes
Paper
Scissors
Pencil
Paste
Old shirt
Teacher-made coat pattern (see page 138)

Materials Preparation

1. Determine the size of the paint paper. Make an oaktag coat pattern by enlarging the Student Activity Pattern to fit the paint paper.

2. Provide an assortment of paper larger than the coat pattern.

Directions for File Folder Activities

Activity 1

The student traces the coat pattern on paper and cuts it out.

Activity 2

The student pastes the coat onto the paint paper. He or she paints Harry wearing his new coat. The student may also paint background.

Takeoff

1. Creative writing. Pretend you are Harry the dog. Write a thank-you letter to Grandma for your new coat.

2. Make posters or want ads for the return of Harry's coat.

3. Make nesting bags for the birds in the spring. Each student will need one recycled small mesh bag with at least ¼" inch holes (the kind used for packaging fruits and vegetables). He or she will also need one pipe cleaner. Prepare a collection of nesting materials (encourage the students to bring in string, yarn, cotton, fabric scraps, ribbon, leaves, and so on). Each student will fill his or her mesh bag about three-quarters full of small pieces of nesting materials. He or she can weave and tie the bag shut with a pipe cleaner. The students can hang their bags on trees in the spring. Encourage the students to observe the birds who visit their bags. They may wish to share their observations with the class.

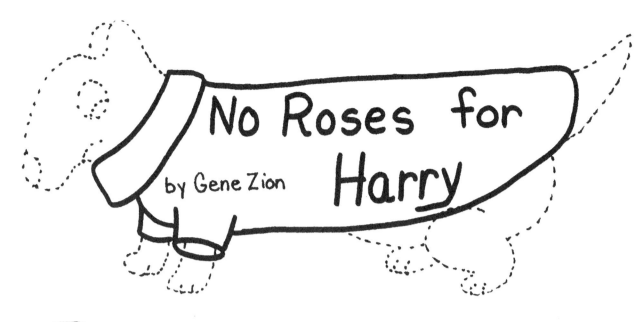

No Roses for Harry

by Gene Zion

1 Trace the coat pattern. Cut it out.

coat pattern

2 Make Harry in his new coat.

Paste

No Roses for Harry
File Folder Directions

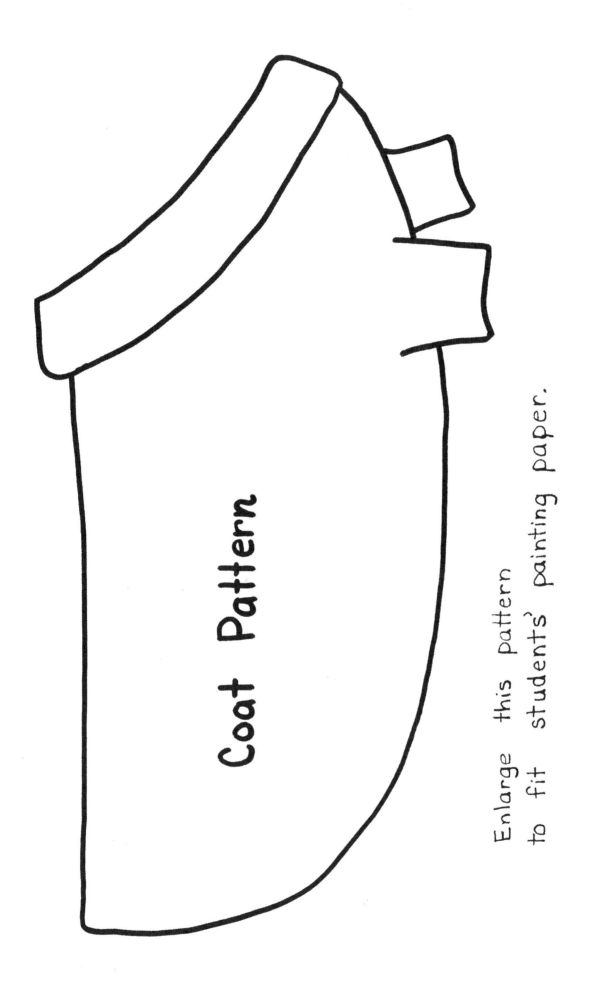

Coat Pattern

Enlarge this pattern to fit students' painting paper.

TEACHER'S DIRECTIONS FOR *MRS. DUNPHY'S DOG* CENTER

Skills Reading, computer, using reference materials, creative writing, fine-motor coordination

Materials Needed

Book: O'Neill, Catherine, *Mrs. Dunphy's Dog,* New York: Viking Penguin, 1987

Copies of Student Activity Page (see page 142)

Computer and printer

Newspapers

Scissors

Crayons

Paste

Materials Preparation

1. Determine whether or not you want the students to put the mounted newspaper articles on a bulletin board or compile them into a class book. Emphasize choosing newspaper articles that James (Mrs. Dunphy's dog) would like to read.

2. The students may use a computer with newspaper/newsletter software and printer to generate a newspaper story for a dog. If a computer and printer are not available, the student may use the Student Activity Page to complete his or her story.

3. Options for the younger student:
   a. Cut out and paste into prestapled books newspaper or magazine pictures and stories that James would like to read.
   b. Draw a picture on the Student Activity Page and dictate a story to an aide for copying onto the page.

Directions for File Folder Activities

Activity 1

The student cuts out and pastes a newspaper article onto paper per your directions.

Activity 2

The student writes a newspaper story for a dog per your directions.

Takeoff

1. Make a class or school newspaper. The Student Activity Page may be used by students to create a day or week of classroom or school-wide news. Assemble pages into book form and duplicate one copy per student or family. After examining a real newspaper, your students may decide to include additional sections such as sports, entertainment, editorial, comics, want ads, and movie, video, or book reviews.

2. Prepare a collection of newspaper photographs (cut out, glue, mount on tagboard, and laminate). The students could write stories about the photographs. Younger students could create stories and tell about them.

3. Read aloud *Mrs. Dunphy's Dog* and discuss the books that James liked to read. Make a list of additional dog books that James might enjoy.

Mrs. Dunphy's Dog

by Catherine O'Neill

1   Cut out a newspaper article. Paste it on paper.

2   Write a newspaper story for a dog.

I ♡ reading!

Write a front page news story for James, Mrs. Dunphy's dog, to read.

price ↗

name of the newspaper ↗

day of week   month ↗   date, year ↗

head lines

by
STAFF REPORTER (your name) ↗

PHOTO BY_____

picture caption ↗

Mrs. Dunphy's Dog
Student Activity Page

TEACHER'S DIRECTIONS FOR *MINE WILL, SAID JOHN* CENTER

Skills Reading, speaking, creating, fine-motor coordination, science

Materials Needed

    Book: Griffith, Helen V., *Mine Will, Said John,* New York: Greenwillow Books, 1980

    Copies of Student Activity Pages on oaktag (see pages 146 and 147)

    One 6″ × 7½″ piece of netting per student (recycled fruit or vegetable bag)

    One 6″ × 12″ piece each of pink, blue, and yellow cellophane per student

    Scissors

    Straight pins

    Carpet sample

    Tape

    Teacher-made set of animals

    Teacher-made cage

    Overhead projector

Materials Preparation

1. Make a set of animals. Put an animal Student Activity Page 1 on top of a carpet sample. Use a straight pin to poke through the dotted lines on the animals, then cut out the animals.

2. Make an animal cage. Cut out the cage on the Student Activity Page 2. Tape a piece of netting to the outer edges of the cage.

3. Demonstrate the proper techniques for retelling the story by using the animals on the overhead projector. Overlap the appropriate colors of cellophane over the cage to show the changes in the chameleon.

Directions for File Folder Activities

Activity 1

The student makes the animal props for the story.

Activity 2

The student practices retelling the story on the overhead projector. Optional: Retell the story at home using the props inside a lighted lamp with a white shade.

Takeoff

1. Discuss the properties of light. Mixing the colors of cellophane made different colors. The cellophane is "transparent" because it allows light to pass through. The animals are "opaque" because light will not pass through. The students may enjoy other color-mixing experiments.

2. The students may enjoy retelling other stories using props for the overhead projector or flannel-backed pictures for the flannelboard. (See the last section of this book for more details.)

3. Make silhouettes (profiles) of students on black paper mounted onto white paper. Discuss how early Americans used the silhouette technique to capture their profiles before the invention of the camera.

Mine Will, Said John
by Helen V. Griffith

1 Make the props for the story.

carpet

2

Now practice re-telling the story.

gerbil

chameleon

frog

puppy

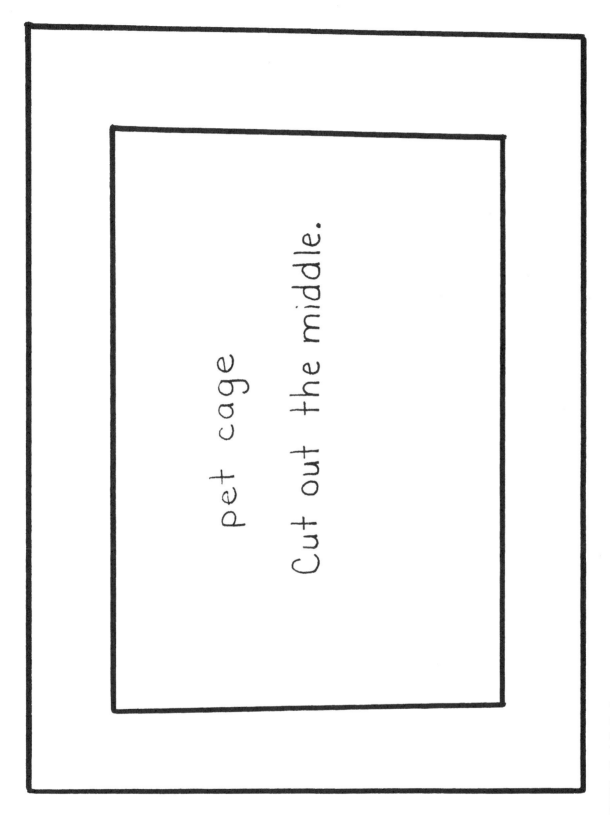

pet cage

Cut out the middle.

TEACHER'S DIRECTIONS FOR *TALLYHO, PINKERTON!* CENTER

Skills Reading, science, using reference materials, fine-motor coordination

Materials Needed

   Book: Kellogg, Steven, *Tallyho, Pinkerton!*, New York: Dial Press, 1982
   Copies of Student Activity Page (see page 150)
   Pencil

Materials Preparation

Determine how the students will complete the activity. You may wish to:

a. Make a set of identification reference cards (such as 3″ × 5″ index cards) naming all the birds and mammals in the book. The students may arrange the cards in alphabetical order and write them on the Student Activity Page.

b. Write beginning and ending letters on the Student Activity Page lists prior to duplicating.

c. Encourage younger students to draw pictures of the birds and mammals on paper folded into an appropriate number of boxes (you may want to make an example paper).

Directions for File Folder Activities

Activity 1

The student will look carefully for the mammals and birds in the book.

Activity 2

The student will help the girl in the book do her homework by completing the Student Activity Page per your directions.

Takeoff

   1. Make a class mural about the book *Tallyho, Pinkerton!*

   2. Creative writing. Students can write letters to the little girl's teacher in the book *Tallyho, Pinkerton!* explaining why her homework was not completed.

   3. Read aloud the book *Keep Looking!* by Millicent Selsam and Joyce Hunt (New York: Macmillan, 1989). Discuss and list on a chart book the twenty-one birds and animals in the book, as well as animal homes and habitats. Divide the class into small groups to research various animals and birds using reference materials.

Tallyho, Pinkerton !
by Steven Kellogg

1 Look for the mammals and birds in the book.

2 Help the girl do her homework.

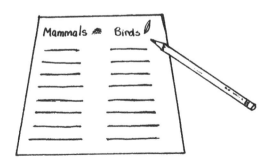

Tallyho, Pinkerton!
File Folder Directions

Mammals: _fur_

1. _____
2. _____
3. _____
4. _____
5. _____
6. _____
7. _____
8. _____
?. _____
   name

Birds: _feathers_

1. _____
2. _____
3. _____
4. _____
5. _____
6. _____
7. _____
8. _____
?. _____
   name

or

Put your name on the right list!

Tallyho, Pinkerton!
Student Activity Page

TEACHER'S DIRECTIONS FOR *DOG FOR A DAY* CENTER

Skills Reading, art, math, speaking, fine-motor coordination, teacher's choice

Materials Needed

Book: Gackenbach, Dick, *Dog for a Day,* New York: Clarion Books, 1987

Copies of Student Activity Page (see page 154)

One box per student such as a shoe box, tissue box, or cereal box

One piece of oaktag (approximately 3½″ × 12″) per student

A collection of junk materials such as cardboard tubes, lids, spools, straws, pipe cleaners, cardboard strips, wallpaper, assorted colors and sizes of construction paper

Tape

Pencil

Scissors

Teacher-made "changing box"

Teacher-made set of Changing Cards

Materials Preparation

1. Make a "changing box" as pictured on the file folder directions. Cut two rectangles 3½″ × ¾″ in the front of the box. Insert a narrow strip of oaktag approximately 3½″ × 12″ through the top ("in") rectangle and out the bottom ("out") with the ends protruding. Tape the top edge of the strip to the upper part of the "in" rectangle and the bottom edge to the lower part of the "out" rectangle. (You may need to adjust the length of the oaktag strip to enable the cards to reverse.) Emphasize student use of the materials from the junk collection to make his or her box unique.

2. You will need to determine the skill you wish to reinforce or review. Some ideas are

   a. Number families such as 7 (3 + 4 changes to 4 + 3, 5 + 2 changes to 2 + 5, and so on).
   b. Combinations of numbers equaling one number such as 3 + 4 changes to 6 + 1.
   c. Contractions, for example, *you will* changes to *you'll.*
   d. Opposite words, for example, *big* changes to *little.*
   e. Initial consonants, for example, *bananas* changes to another word beginning with *b.*
   f. Dog riddle changes to answer.

3. Determine the number of changing cards you wish the students to make, then duplicate the appropriate number of Student Activity Pages.

4. Use a copy of the Student Activity Page to make an example set of changing cards with the appropriate skill. Emphasize writing the problem such as 3 + 4 on the front of the card and what it will change into (4 + 3) on the back of the card. Insert the cards into the changing box to demonstrate this activity.

Directions for File Folder Activities

Activity 1

The student makes a changing box per your directions.

Activity 2

The student uses the Student Activity Page to make changing cards per your directions. Optional: The student may use his or her changing box and cards with a friend.

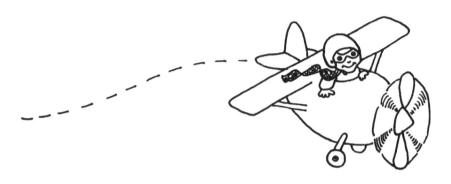

Takeoff

1. The students may create other skill cards (refer to materials preparation) to be used with their changing boxes.

2. The students can write and illustrate books showing the people and objects Sidney changed in *Dog for a Day,* such as: baby sister changed into a lamp, a football changed into a toaster, a canary changed into a cat, and Wally changed into Sidney. The students may want to make changes of people and objects in their home or school. ("I wish I could change _____ into a _____ .") The students may want to read their books to another class, as described in "Enjoying Language Arts" at the back of this book.

3. The students can finish this creative writing activity: "If I were a dog for a day, I would . . ."

Dog for a Day
by Dick Gackenbach

Sidney

Wally

1 Make a "Changing Box."

"Junk" for Changing Box

tape

in

out

2 Make cards that will change in the box.

in
change
-o-
matic
OFF

You will write on the front and on the back.

Changing Cards

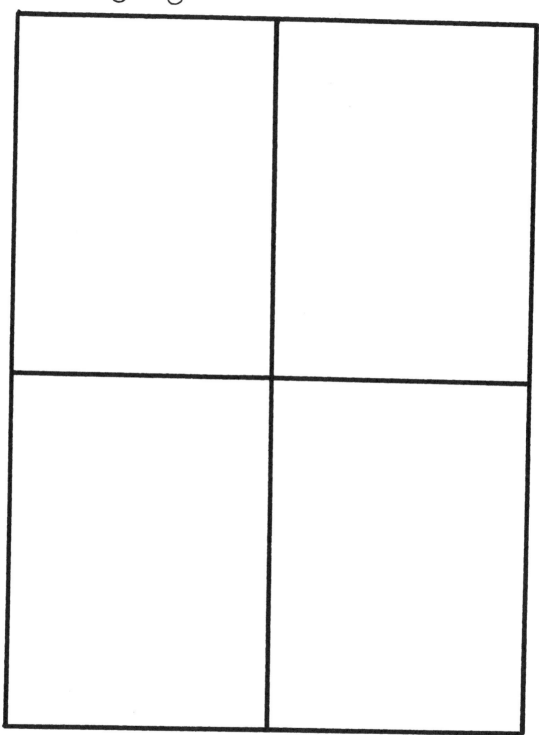

Cut out the cards. Write on the front.
On the back, write what it will change into.

Dog for a Day
Student Activity Page

TEACHER'S DIRECTIONS FOR *GIVE A DOG A BONE* CENTER

Skills Reading, listening, speaking, art, creative writing, fine-motor coordination

Materials Needed

Book: Wildsmith, Brian, *Give a Dog a Bone,* New York: Pantheon Books, 1985
Copies of the Student Activity Page duplicated on heavy paper (see page 158)
Tape recorder
Cassette tape
Two pieces of 3″ × 5″ felt per student
Scissors
Glue
Pencil
Crayons
Stapler and staples
Teacher-made bone pattern
Teacher-made bone book

Materials Preparation

1. Prepare a cassette tape of the book.

2. Make an oaktag bone pattern the same size as the bone on the Student Activity Page and laminate it.

3. Make a bone book:
   a. Use the Student Activity Page for the cover. Draw a dog's head on the cover with crayons.
   b. Make two felt bones. Trace the bone pattern onto two pieces of felt and cut them out. Glue one felt bone on the cover and lay the additional felt bone on top of it.
   c. You will need to determine the number of pages for each book, the way you want it written, and how it should be stapled. Some ideas are to draw pictures and write sentences to sequence the events in the *Give a Dog a Bone* book with the dog and his bone appearing on each page. You may wish to have the student create his or her own story featuring a dog and his bone in a variety of situations. (The student will remove the felt bone from the cover and place it on each page as he or she writes the story.) The student may wish to share his or her book with another class. (See "Enjoying Language Arts" for more details.)

Directions for File Folder Activities

Activity 1

The student listens to the story.

Activity 2

The student makes a book per your directions. Optional: The student may read the book to a friend.

Takeoff

1. Provide a large jar filled with dog bone biscuits. Each student can estimate the number of dog bone biscuits in the jar. After the students have completed their estimations and the total number of bones has been determined, you may wish to use the dog bones for an art project. The students could create dogs from assorted sizes and colors of paper. A dog bone biscuit could be glued to each dog's mouth.

2. Make a bone fishing game. Give each student a dog bone pattern to trace several times on construction paper, then cut out the bones. Next he or she copies reading vocabulary words, math problems, or spelling words onto the bones. The student can use a stapler to put two staples in the form of an X on each bone. He or she may make a fishing pole at home by attaching one end of a piece of string to a ruler and the opposite end to a magnet. Then the student can lay the bones on the floor and use the pole to fish for the bones.

Give a Dog a Bone
by Brian Wildsmith

1  Listen to the book.

2 Now make your own bone book.

Give a Dog a Bone
File Folder Directions

Give a Dog a Bone

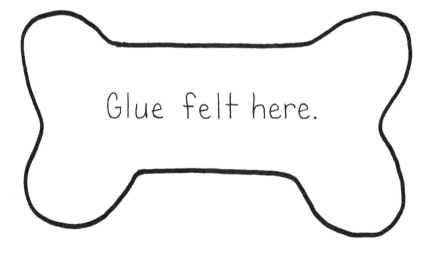

Glue felt here.

name _____

Dogs
Enrichment Activities

Whingdingdoggie

Surf's up!

TEACHER'S DIRECTIONS FOR "DOGS" ENRICHMENT ACTIVITIES

"Dogs" Group Activity

As a culminating activity to the "Dogs" language arts unit, schedule CANINE CAPERS events.

Send the Canine Capers letter to parents at least one week prior to the Canine Capers events.

The following are suggested Canine Caper events activities:

1. Share *Doggy Tales* prior to sending them home.

2. Discuss The Dog Research Activity project (arrange for the Dog Research Activity Page to be returned a few days prior to the Canine Capers events).

3. Graph the results of the Dog Research Activity Project.

4. Play Spelling Bingo.

5. Plan a "Doggone Good Read-In" as described in the parent Canine Capers letter. In the morning provide materials such as newspaper, scrap paper, masking tape, and so on. Each student will convert his or her desk into a doghouse with a dog's name on it. (You may wish to give prizes for the most creative, best name, etc.) In the afternoon, each student will take his or her sleeping bag or blanket, pillow, dog books, and "doggie" bag of snacks into his or her doghouse and read silently for one hour. After the hour, divide students into pairs or small groups. Encourage each student to share the highlights of one of the favorite dog books he or she read during the "Doggone Good Read-In."

6. Invite the students' parents or willing adults to bring the student's dog to school at a designated time. (Refer to Canine Capers letter.) If possible, plan to take your students to a prearranged outside area when the dogs come to visit. It works well to have the students sit in a large circle on the ground. The student with his or her dog can take a turn standing in the center of the circle. He or she may tell about the dog and answer questions about it.

7. You may wish to schedule a veterinarian to talk to your students regarding proper dog health care.

8. Videotape the Canine Capers events. (If possible, arrange for a parent to do it.) The students may take the videotape home to share with their families, as described in "Enjoying Language Arts" at the back of this book.

"Dogs" Read-at-Home Activity

Encourage the students to read dog books by different authors. Determine the number of books you wish the student to read during a two- or three-week period. The student records the title, author, and date of the books read on the "Dogs" Read-at-home Activity Page.

"Dogs" Read-at-Home Award

Duplicate the award onto colored paper. Give the award to each child who reads the required number of books and returns the completed "Dogs" Read-at-Home Activity Page.

"Dogs" Spelling Activity

Play Spelling Bingo. Students copy their spelling list in random order on the Spelling Activity Page. (This activity is good for review words, too, because there are spaces for twenty-four words.) A duplicate set of spelling words is written on cards and placed in a container. A student or the teacher pulls and reads aloud one card from the container at a time. The remaining students cover the word with a marker. When one student has five correct words in a row, he or she calls "Bingo!" Then the student reads and/or spells the words aloud to verify his or her bingo. Don't forget to sing the song about the Farmer and his dog Bingo. You may also want to sing:

> There are twenty-six letters of the alphabet
> And five of them are vowels,
> A, E, I, O, U
> A, E, I, O, U
> A, E, I, O, U
> And sometimes Y and W!

"Dogs" Creative Writing Activity

1. *Doggy Tales*. The student will write a bedtime story for a dog. Encourage the student to write a story about something a dog might like to hear. Some ideas include: What do dogs like to think about? Do you know a fairy tale or nursery rhyme that you could change to please a dog's point of view? Who's point of view could you write the story from (yours, a cat's, a flea's, a dog's)?

2. Stories may be written in preassembled books. Determine the method of writing books. Younger students may dictate stories to an aide. Use the "Dogs" Creative Writing Book Plate for a book plate that the student will complete and paste inside his or her front cover.

3. The *Doggy Tale* books may be stored in the class library. The students may check out, take home, and read the books to family dogs, other pets, and other family members. A comment sheet similar to the one given in "Enjoying Language Arts" may be filled out. You may want to add the following question to the comment sheet: What did the dog do when this story was read to him or her?

"Dogs" Research Activity

Duplicate the page for older students to complete independently within seven to ten days. Younger students may complete the activity with parental help. Arrange a time such as Canine Capers for the students to share their research page.

"Dogs" Summary Page

Read aloud *The Whingdingdilly* by Bill Peet (Boston: Houghton-Mifflin, 1970). Duplicate the "Crazy, Mixed-Up Dog" Page. The student draws a picture of a dog, emphasizing body parts from the dogs in this chapter. The student describes the features of the dog he or she has created. Some ideas are: "I chose the tail from Clifford," "I chose the legs from Pinkerton," and so on.

 **Canine Capers**

Date _____

Dear Parent,

As a culminating activity for our "Dog" language arts unit we will have Canine Capers events on _____.

On that morning, the students will share the *Doggy Tales* which they have written at school. They will also discuss their Dog Research Activity projects. (Thank you for helping with the project. Please remind your child to return the Dog Research Activity Page on _____ .) As a math activity, the students will graph information from the Dog Research project.

Later in the morning, the students will use newspapers, paper, and recycled materials to change their desks into doghouses.

In the afternoon, we will have a "Doggone Good Read-In." The students will stay in their doghouses to read their favorite dog books silently for one hour. In order to make the "Doggone Good Read-In" more fun, each child should bring:

1. Three or more of his or her favorite dog books (be sure that his or her name is written in the book or on a book bag)
2. A sleeping bag/blanket and a pillow
3. A snack in a "doggie" bag, for example, grapes, carrots, celery, cookie, and a boxed juice drink (no soda pop)

Many students have wanted to bring their dogs to school this year. As the final event of our Canine Capers, dogs accompanied by an adult are welcome to visit at _____ . Videotapes or photographs of your dog may be sent if it is inconvenient to bring your dog to school.

I will plan to videotape many of the Canine Capers events. Your child will have an opportunity to share the tape with your family.

Thank you for your continued support.

Sincerely,

_____
Your child's teacher

"Dogs" Read-at-Home Activity Page

Return by _____

Date _____

Dear Parent,

    During the next two weeks, our language arts learning centers will feature dog books.
    Encourage your child to read _____ dog books by several different authors. He or she will need to record the titles, the authors, and the dates the books were read on the attached Read-at-Home Activity Page.
    Each child who reads the required number of books and completes the activity page will receive an award. Please return the completed activity page on _____ .
    You may enjoy reading some of your favorite dog books aloud with your child.
    Thank you for your help with this activity.

Sincerely,

_____
Your child's teacher

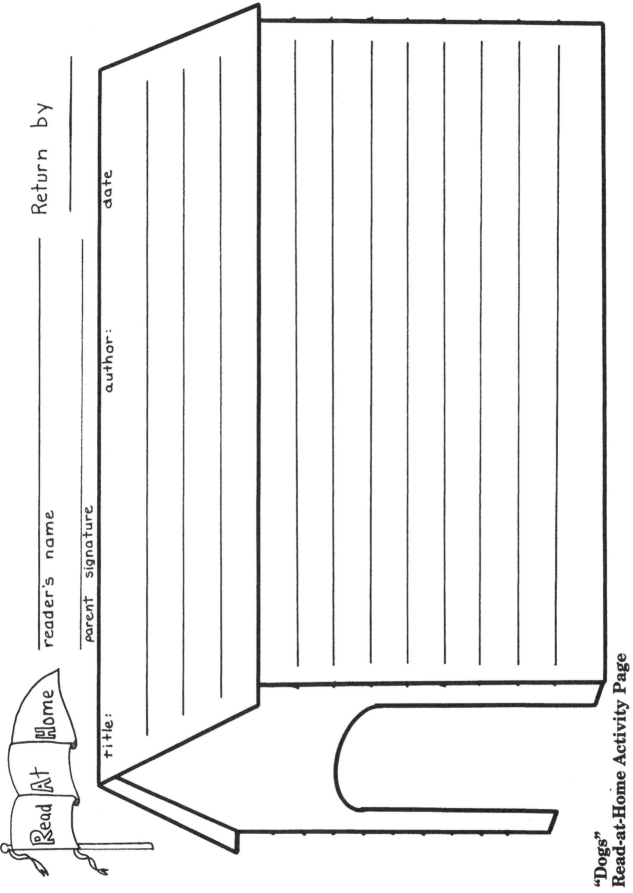

Return by
_____
date

author:

reader's name
_____

parent signature
_____

title:

Read At Home

"Dogs"
Read-at-Home Activity Page

"Dogs"
Read-at-Home Award

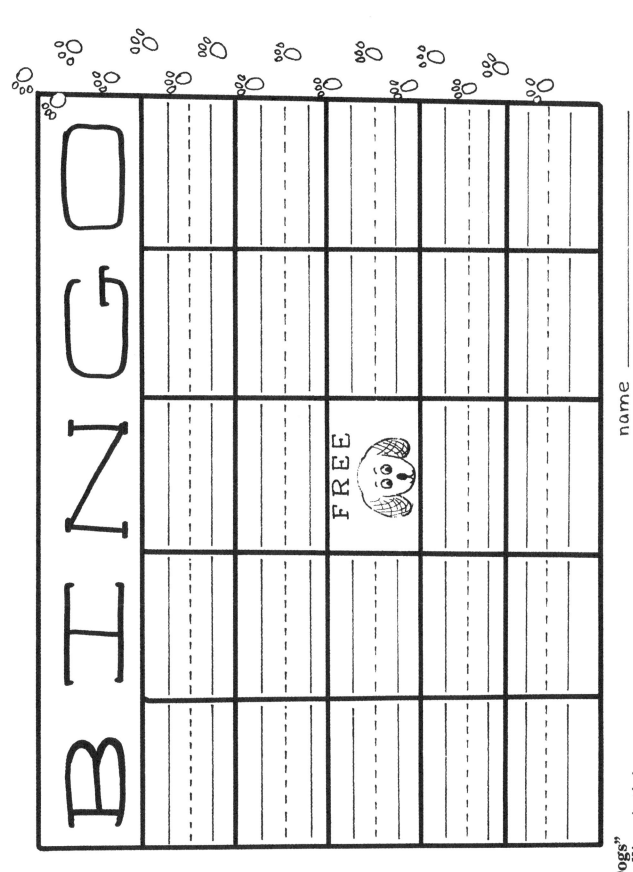

B I N G O

FREE

name _____

"Dogs"
Spelling Activity

Doggy Tale

This book was written for a special dog named _____ to help him/her have sweet dreams!

title _____
author_____
illustrator_____
date written _____

"Dogs"
Creative Writing Book Plate

Name: _____   **Return on:** _____

Research your pet dog, a dog you know, or a dog you would like to have for a pet.

1. Dog's name: _____

2. Who selected the name? _____

3. Dog's owner: _____

4. Dog's age: _____ How long has dog lived with owner? _____

5. What breed is the dog? _____

6. Where did the owner get the dog? _____

7. Who takes care of the dog's needs?

   a. Food: _____

      What food does the dog like? _____

      What food does the dog dislike? _____

   b. Exercise: _____

   c. Grooming: _____

   d. Love: _____

   e. Shelter: _____

      Does the dog live inside or outside? _____

   f. Veterinarian visits: _____

8. Has the dog attended obedience school? _____

9. Who trained the dog? _____

10. Does the dog know any tricks? _____

11. Does the dog have any special toys? _____

12. Who are the dog's friends? _____
13. Draw a picture of the dog on the back of this page or attach a photograph of the dog.
14. You may write more about the dog on the back of this page or on an additional page if you wish.

"Dogs"
Research Activity Page

Crazy, Mixed-up Dog

nose ❧ home ❧ color ❧ guard ❧ travel ❧ paws ❧ size ❧ obedience ❧ run ❧

special talents ❧ vacation ❧ tag ❧

adventures ❧ problems ❧ owners ❧

❧ bark ❧ tail ❧ food ❧ large ❧ fetch ❧ body ❧ friends ❧ ears ❧ birds ❧

_____

_____

_____

_____

_____

_____

_____

_____

_____

_____

_____

Name

"Dogs"
Summary Page

American Tall Tales and Legends

Paul Bunyan

JOHN HENRY

Pecos Bill

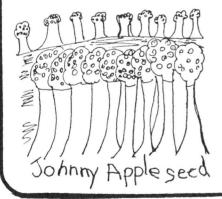

Johnny Appleseed

Little Gopher

171

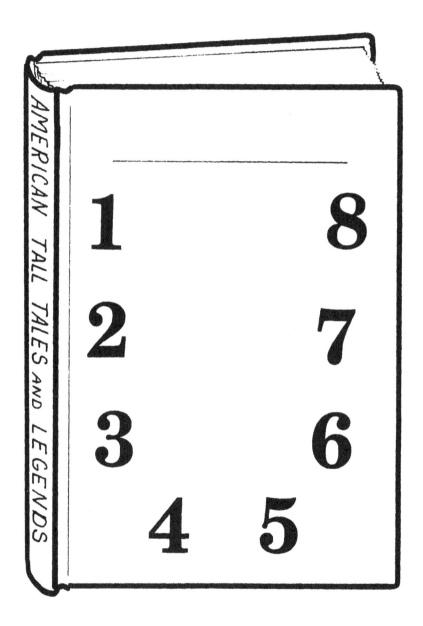

"American Tall Tales and Legends"
Center Marker

Date _____

Dear Parent,

   "American Tall Tales and Legends" is the theme of our language arts learning centers during the next two weeks. Each center will feature a different tale or legend which may be familiar to you.

   An old favorite, *Rip Van Winkle*, will be sleeping on our bulletin board. Each day his beard will grow longer. The class will make predictions and inventions for the future. Please help all of our "inventors" by sending unwanted items (cardboard tubes, boxes of various sizes, lids, foam trays from meat or produce, and so on) for this center.

   At the *John Henry* center your child will make a hammer and spike matching game. He or she may want to play this game with someone in your family.

   Your child will need a shoe box or facial tissue box to create a diorama at the *Johnny Appleseed* center.

   Our listening center will be inside *Paul Bunyan's* tent. Your child will have the opportunity to wear "Paul's shirt," listen to the story, and create a "Babe the Blue Ox" pin design.

   Encourage your child to tell you the story about *Pecos Bill* using his or her mobile for a reference.

   Your child will make thirteen clay cookies at *The Baker's Dozen* center. He or she may wish to paint the cookies at home. Please send a small cookie cutter (less than 2″) with your child's name written on it with a permanent marker. As a math activity, your child will also estimate objects in jars at this center, then count them. You may wish to extend this activity at home.

   Please send the shoe box/facial tissue box, cookie cutter, and recycled unwanted items by _____ .

   Thank you for your continued support,

Sincerely,

_____
Your child's teacher

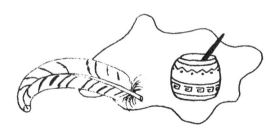

HOTLINE FROM

Parent ——— TO ——— School

Date _____

Dear Parent,

    I would appreciate any feedback you or your child may have regarding the "American Tall Tales and Legends" learning centers: *Rip Van Winkle, The Legend of the Indian Paintbrush, John Henry, Pecos Bill, Johnny Appleseed, Paul Bunyan, Hiawatha,* and *The Baker's Dozen.*
    Please use this page for comments and return it to me by _____ .

Sincerely,

_____

Your child's teacher

Date _____

Dear _____ ,

"AMERICAN TALL TALES AND LEGENDS" LEARNING CENTERS LIST

These learning centers feature books about American tall tales and legends.

Rip Van Winkle Center

(a bulletin board is used with this center)

Skills Reading, creative writing, creating, fine-motor coordination

Activities
1. Glue cotton balls onto Rip Van Winkle's beard on the bulletin board.
2. Make a prediction and an invention for the future.

The Legend of the Indian Paintbrush Center

Skills Reading, art, using reference materials, fine-motor coordination

Activities
1. Paint Little Gopher's sunset.
2. Make a "skin," then draw and label Indian signs on it.

John Henry Center (Open-Ended Activity)

Skills Reading, speaking, fine-motor coordination, using reference materials, teacher's choice

Activities
1. Make a matching hammer and spike game using the Student Activity Pages.
2. Play your game with a friend.

Pecos Bill Center

Skills Reading, speaking, creating, fine-motor coordination

Activities
1. Make a mobile about Pecos Bill.
2. Tell a friend about Pecos Bill using your mobile as a reference.

Johnny Appleseed Center

Skills Reading, speaking, creative writing, art, fine-motor coordination

Activities
1. Make a diorama about Johnny Appleseed.
2. Write a story about Johnny Appleseed on the Student Activity Page.

Paul Bunyan Center

Skills Reading, listening, fine-motor coordination

Activities
1. Put on Paul's shirt, go inside the tent, and listen to the cassette tape of the book.
2. Make a pin design of Babe the Blue Ox in the tent.

Hiawatha Center

Skills Reading, computer, creating, fine-motor coordination, science

Activities
1. Use the computer and printer. Type the words on the pages and make your book.
2. Draw the animal pictures in your book.

The Baker's Dozen Center

Skills Reading, math, creating, art, fine-motor coordination

Activities
1. Estimate and then count the objects.
2. Make a baker's dozen of cookies.

"AMERICAN TALL TALES AND LEGENDS" CENTER MARKER

Distribute copies of the "American Tall Tales and Legends" center marker (refer to page 172) to the students. The students can color, cut out, and place their center markers near the "American Tall Tales and Legends" learning centers.

TEACHER'S DIRECTIONS FOR *RIP VAN WINKLE* CENTER

Skills Reading, creative writing, creating, fine-motor coordination

Materials Needed

A book about Rip Van Winkle, such as: Gipson, Morrell, *Rip Van Winkle,* Garden City, New York: Doubleday, 1987; Locker, Thomas, *Rip Van Winkle,* New York: Dial Books, 1988; York, Carol Beach, *Washington Irving's Rip Van Winkle,* Mahwah, NJ: Troll Associates, 1980

Bulletin board

Copies of Student Activity Page (see page 180)

Pencil

Crayons

Cotton balls

Masking tape

Glue

Scissors

A collection of junk materials, such as cardboard tubes, boxes of various sizes, plastic bottles, lids, spools, foam trays from meat or produce, straws, cardboard strips, assorted colors and sizes of construction paper

Materials Preparation

1. Prepare a bulletin board as pictured on the File Folder Direction Page. Use posterboard to make Rip Van Winkle (laminate him for reuse). Attach a paper beard outline to the posterboard beard. The students will glue cotton balls onto the paper beard starting at the chin (the beard will grow longer each day). When you are finished with the bulletin board, the paper beard may be disposed of. You will need to determine the number of cotton balls you wish to have each student use.

2. Establish background about predictions.

Directions for File Folder Activities

Activity 1

The student will glue cotton balls onto Rip Van Winkle's beard on the bulletin board.

Activity 2

The student will complete the information on the Student Activity Page. (You may wish to compile the pages into a class traveling book, as described in "Enjoying Language Arts.") The student will use junk materials to make an invention for the future.

Takeoff

1. Give students an opportunity to contrast their present lives with the past by examining photographs in old magazines, catalogs, or encyclopedia yearbooks. (These might be obtained inexpensively from flea markets, garage sales, library book sales, or auctions). The students may bring in any of these materials to share.

2. If there is a new public building under construction in your area, perhaps your students could compile a class list of predictions to place in the cornerstone. Visit a museum, church, or public building to view the contents of a cornerstone that has been opened.

3. To increase your students' awareness of the passage of time, you may want to introduce a time line.

Rip Van Winkle

by Washington Irving

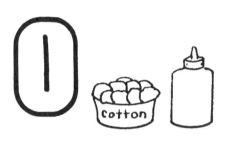

1

What will happen in 20 years?

year: [20__]

Glue cotton balls on his beard.

2 Make a prediction

My Prediction for the Future
My

and an invention for the future.

"Junk" for Inventions for the Future

glue

Rip Van Winkle
File Folder Directions

My Prediction for the Future

My name _____

Today's date _____ , _____
               month   date   year

20 years from
today it will be _____ , _____
               month   date   year

I am _____ years old today.

  +   20

I will be _____ years old in 20 years!

My invention for the future is _____

I predict it will _____
_____
_____

TEACHER'S DIRECTIONS FOR *THE LEGEND OF THE INDIAN PAINTBRUSH* CENTER

Skills Reading, art, using reference materials, fine-motor coordination

Materials Needed

> Book: de Paola, Tomie, *The Legend of the Indian Paintbrush* New York: G. P. Putnam's Sons, 1988
>
> Easel
>
> Paintbrushes
>
> Several sets of watercolor paints (red, orange, and yellow. Optional: pink)
>
> Paper
>
> Old shirt
>
> An assortment of water-base, fine-point marking pens
>
> One recycled brown paper bag (approximately 12″ × 17″) per student
>
> Teacher-made example painting
>
> Teacher-made example "skin"
>
> Teacher-made Indian sign reference chart

Materials Preparation

1. Paint an example of a sunset stressing colors in the following top to bottom order: red, orange, yellow.

2. Make an Indian sign reference chart. Some resource books are *Indian Sign Language* by Robert Hofsinde (New York: William Morrow and Co., 1956), *The Complete Book of Indian Crafts and Lore* by Ben W. Hunt (New York: Golden Press, 1954), *Indian and Camp Handicraft* by W. Ben Hunt (New York: Bruce Publishing Co., 1938), and *Wolf Cub Scout Book* (Irving, TX: Boy Scouts of America, 1986).

3. Make an example "skin." Wad up a brown paper bag several times and flatten it out to create a soft and wrinkled appearing skin. Use marking pens to draw and label Indian signs on the "skin," referring to your reference chart. Determine the number of signs you wish to have the students make.

Directions for File Folder Activities

Activity 1

The student will paint Little Gopher's sunset.

Activity 2

The student will make a "skin" from a bag per your example. He or she will draw and label Indian signs on the skin using the Indian signs chart as a reference.

Takeoff

1. Your students may enjoy experimenting with natural materials to obtain colors such as the American Indians did. Berries or roots may be mashed to obtain liquids of various colors. The students could use the liquids on paper, clay pottery, or amulets. Perhaps a local artist would be able to help with obtaining and using natural materials.

2. Animal hides are mentioned in *The Legend of the Indian Paintbrush.* Different hides could be collected and contrasted, for example, a cowhide wallet, sheepskin slippers, deerskin gloves, and leather sports balls.

3. The students can create rebus stories using words and Indian signs.

The Legend of the Indian Paintbrush

Retold by Tomie de Paola

1 Paint Little Gopher's sunset.

sponge

water

2 Make a skin from a bag.

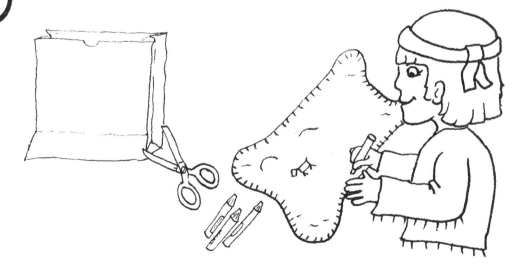

The Legend of the Indian Paintbrush
File Folder Directions

TEACHER'S DIRECTIONS FOR *JOHN HENRY* CENTER

Skills Reading, speaking, fine-motor coordination, using reference materials, teacher's choice

Materials Needed

> A book about John Henry, such as Keats, Ezra Jack, *John Henry,* New York: Alfred A. Knopf, 1987; Naden, C. J., *John Henry,* Mahwah, NJ: Troll Associates, 1980
>
> Copies of Student Activity Pages run on construction paper (see pages 187 and 188)
>
> Scissors
>
> Pencil
>
> One envelope per student
>
> Teacher-made reference chart

Materials Preparation

To make a reference chart, use a copy of the hammer Student Activity Page 1 to review or reinforce a skill such as contractions, opposite words, color words and colors, numerals and names of numerals, or math problems. If you prefer math problems, write the problems on the hammers. Laminate the chart.

Directions for File Folder Activities

Activity 1

The student makes a matching hammer and spike game. He or she copies your reference chart on a hammer Student Activity Page 1, then completes the work on the spike Student Activity page 2. For example, when solving math problems, the student could write the problem on the hammer and the answer on a spike. He or she cuts out the hammers and the spikes.

Activity 2

The student lays the hammers and the spikes on the floor. He or she plays the game with a friend by taking turns matching the hammers with the appropriate spikes. Then the student puts the game into an envelope.

Takeoff

1. You may want to research several books about John Henry to find songs about him. Your class may enjoy singing them. Perhaps a music teacher would be willing to help you with the songs.

2. A student who needs manipulatives for subtraction may cup his or her hand over a table to make a "tunnel" like John Henry's. Using beans, the student can subtract from the group by putting them in the tunnel and counting the remaining beans.

John Henry

1 Make a game.

2 Play the game with a friend.

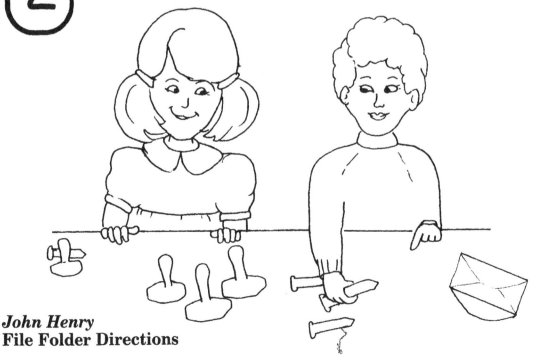

John Henry
File Folder Directions

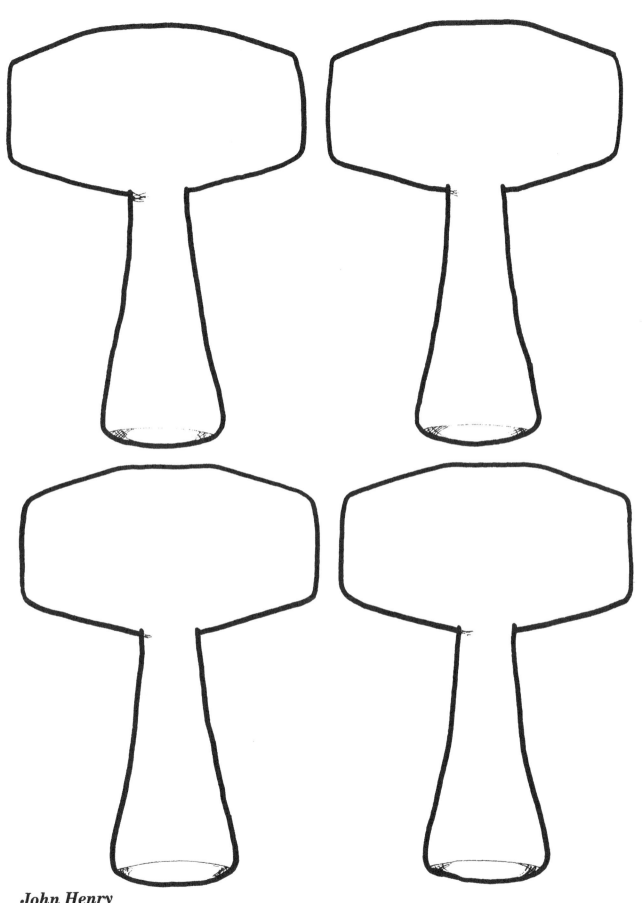

John Henry
Student Activity Page 1

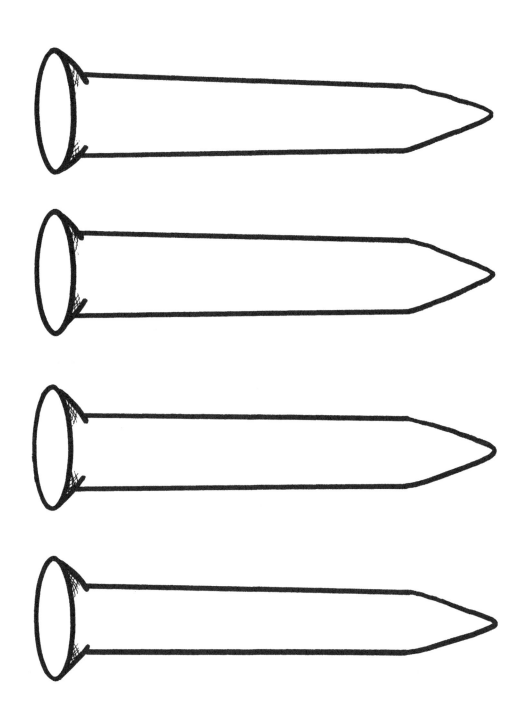

TEACHER'S DIRECTIONS FOR *PECOS BILL* CENTER

Skills Reading, speaking, creating, fine-motor coordination

Materials Needed

> A book about Pecos Bill such as: Dewey, Ariane, *Pecos Bill*, New York: Greenwillow Books, 1983; Kellogg, Steven, *Pecos Bill*, New York: William Morrow, 1986
>
> Copies of the Student Activity Page (see page 192)
>
> One paper plate (9″ diameter) per student
>
> One 9″ × 12″ piece of brown construction paper per student
>
> One 5′ piece of yarn or string per student
>
> Ruler
>
> Paper puncher
>
> Scissors
>
> Crayons
>
> Pencil
>
> Paste
>
> Teacher-made hat pattern (see page 193)

Materials Preparation

1. Duplicate the hat pattern on oaktag, cut it out, and laminate it.

2. You may want to make an example Pecos Bill mobile. Discuss pictures the students may want to draw about the Pecos Bill story. (The student may draw pictures on both sides of the mobile pieces if he or she wishes.)

Directions for File Folder Activities

Activity 1

The student will make a mobile about the book:

1. The student traces your hat pattern on brown construction paper, cuts it out, and pastes it on the paper plate.
2. He or she draws Pecos Bill's face on the plate. Then he or she punches four holes around the outer edge of the plate and one hole in the top of the hat with the paper puncher.
3. The student cuts out the shapes on the Student Activity Page. He or she punches a hole in each dot with a paper puncher.
4. Using the book as a reference, he or she draws a picture on the front of each shape. (Optional: He or she may also draw a picture on the back of each shape.)

5. The student measures and cuts the yarn into five pieces (12″).

6. He or she ties one end of each piece of yarn through a hole in the shape. He or she ties the opposite end of the yarn to a hole in the plate.

7. The student may put the remaining piece of yarn through the hole in the hat and tie it to form a loop hanger.

Activity 2

The student tells a friend about Pecos Bill using the mobile as a reference. Optional: The student may wish to tell his or her story to someone in another classroom, as described in the last section of this book.

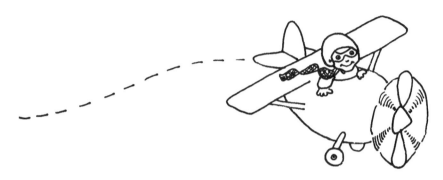

Takeoff

1. The students may enjoy making paper bookmarks featuring some of the animals, characters, or scenes from the Pecos Bill book.

2. Create long paper snakes from construction paper or adding machine tape. Draw a head, then fold the remainder of the snake into sections. The student could write math problems, spelling words, or reading vocabulary words on each section.

Pecos Bill

1 Make a mobile.

2

> And this picture shows the place where Bill...

Tell a friend about Pecos Bill.

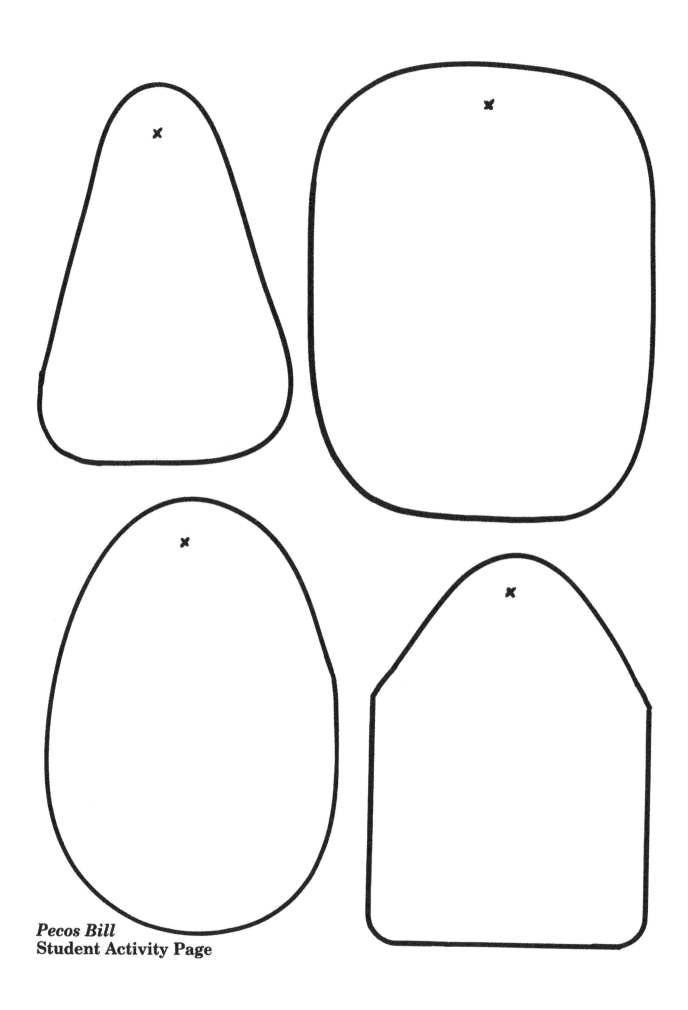

Pecos Bill
Student Activity Page

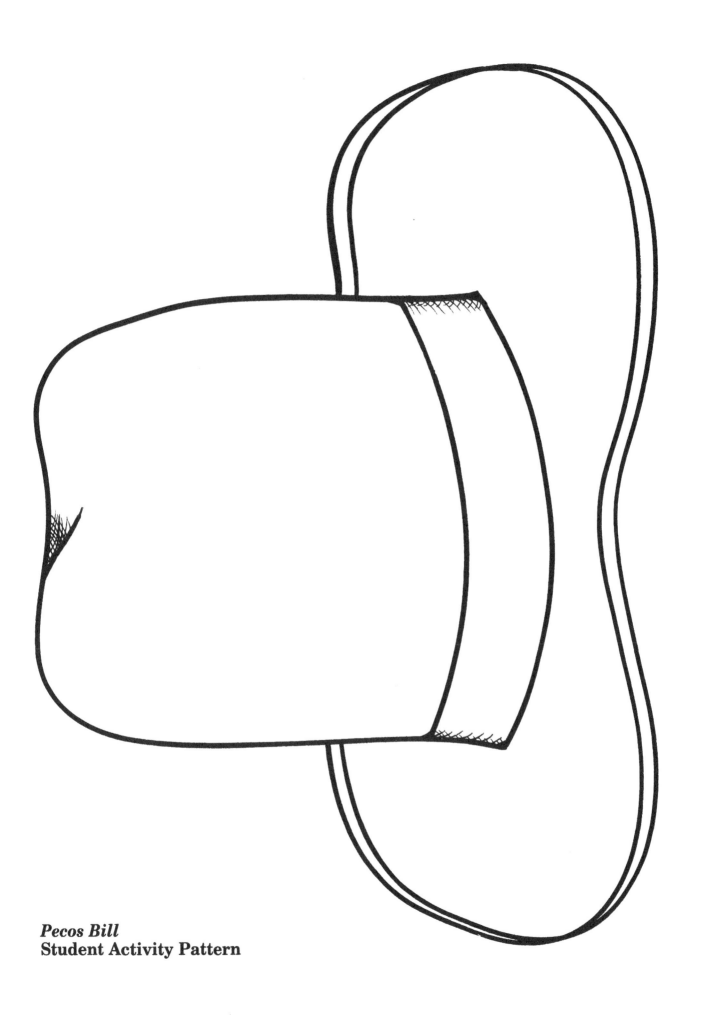

Pecos Bill
Student Activity Pattern

TEACHER'S DIRECTIONS FOR *JOHNNY APPLESEED* CENTER

Skills Reading, speaking, creative writing, art, fine-motor coordination

Materials Needed

A book about Johnny Appleseed, such as: Anderson, J. I., *I Can Read About Johnny Appleseed,* Mahwah, NJ: Troll Associates, 1977; Anderson, La Vere, *Johnny Appleseed,* Champaign, IL: Garrard Publishing Co., 1974; Kellogg, Steven, *Johnny Appleseed,* New York: William Morrow and Co., 1988

Copies of Student Activity Page (see page 197)

An assortment of broad-tipped marking pens

Clay

Cotton balls

A collection of scrap materials such as fabric, wallpaper, construction paper (red, brown, green), tissue paper (red and green), pipe cleaners, and fur

One shoe box or facial-tissue box per student

Pencil

Glue

Scissors (suitable for cutting fabric)

Materials Preparation

You may want to make an example diorama in a shoe box with a few clay animals, cotton-ball clouds, apple trees, and background (marking pens).

Directions for File Folder Activities

Activity 1

The student will make a diorama per your directions.

Activity 2

The student writes a creative story about Johnny Appleseed on the Student Activity Page referring to the vocabulary listed.

Takeoff

1. You may wish to give each student a variety of seeds such as pumpkin, sunflower, popcorn, beans, watermelon, and apple. The student can sort the seeds by size, color, and shape. He or she can then use the seeds to make mosaic pictures.

2. The students may enjoy sprouting seeds in a plastic bag containing a damp paper towel. Seeds which germinate easily could also be planted in soil and grown in the classroom. (Apples grow slowly. Compare their growth with seeds that grow more quickly, such as lima beans.)

3. Visit an orchard or invite an orchard resource person to come into your classroom. Discuss planting, growing, care, and so on, of fruit trees.

Johnny Appleseed

1 Make a diorama.

2 Write about Johnny Appleseed.

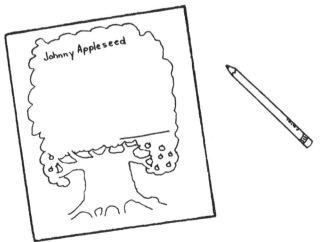

Johnny Appleseed
File Folder Directions

Johnny Appleseed

name _____

animals   traveled   cabin
seeds   settlers
Ohio   knapsack   pan
fruit   help   Indian
walked   blossom
Bible   planted
pouch   orchards
John Chapman   friends
Pennsylvania
apple

Johnny Appleseed
Student Activity Page

TEACHER'S DIRECTIONS FOR *PAUL BUNYAN* CENTER

Skills Reading, listening, fine-motor coordination

Materials Needed

A book about Paul Bunyan, such as: Dolan, Ellen M., and Janet L. Bolinske, *Paul Bunyan,* St. Louis, MO: Milliken Publishing Co., 1987; Kellogg, Steven, *Paul Bunyan,* New York: William Morrow and Co., 1984; Syman, Nanci A., *Paul Bunyan,* Mahwah, NJ: Troll Associates, 1980.

Copies of Student Activity Page (see page 201)

Tape recorder

Cassette tape

One sheet of 9″ × 12″ blue construction paper per student

Straight pins

Stapler and staples

Carpet sample

Small free-standing tent such as a dome tent

Teacher-made Babe poster

Teacher-made sign ("Paul's Tent)

A man's flannel shirt

Materials Preparation

1. Prepare the Student Activity Page in the following way for a pin design: Place the student activity page on top of a piece of construction paper. Staple the top corners of both papers together. Insert a straight pin through the top of the student activity page.

2. Display a large poster of Babe the Blue Ox as featured on the file folder directions page at this center (you may wish to use a bulletin board).

3. Provide a free-standing tent at this center. Optional: Drape a blanket over a desk to create a tent. Attach a sign "Paul's Tent." Place a tape recorder and a carpet sample in the tent.

4. Prepare a cassette tape of the book.

5. Provide a man's flannel shirt for the student to wear at the center. He or she can pretend to be Paul Bunyan.

6. Optional: Establish background regarding the popcorn blizzard which is mentioned in many versions of *Paul Bunyan.* You may wish to provide each student with a small bag of popcorn to eat inside the tent as he or she listens to the story (air-popped corn is best because it is grease free). Place a limited number of bags of popcorn (visible to you) daily outside the tent (this may discourage students from eating more than their allotted amount of popcorn).

Directions for File Folder Activities

Activity 1

The student will put on Paul's shirt, go inside the tent, and listen to the cassette tape of the book.

Activity 2

The student makes a pin design of Babe the Blue Ox in the tent:

1. He or she removes the straight pin from the top of the Student Activity Page.
2. He or she uses the pin to punch holes through the outline of Babe the Blue Ox. (Be sure the student does this work over the carpet sample to protect the floor from pin scratches.)
3. He or she removes the Student Activity Page from the construction paper. (The outline of Babe the Blue Ox will be visible on the construction paper.)

Takeoff

1. Discuss the practice of lumbering during Paul Bunyan's time and the present. Emphasize replacing the earth's resources such as trees and not wasting tree products. Students may wish to plant a tree.

2. Invite a forester or other appropriate resource person to visit your class to discuss the lumbering history of your state or surrounding region.

Paul Bunyan

1 Paul Bunyan's
Lumber Camp

Paul's
Tent

Listen to the story in his tent.

2 Do the pin
design of
Babe the Blue Ox.

Paul Bunyan
File Folder Directions

Babe the Blue Ox

name _____

TEACHER'S DIRECTIONS FOR *HIAWATHA* CENTER

Skills Reading, computer, creating, fine-motor coordination, science

Materials Needed

 Book: Longfellow, Henry Wadsworth, *Hiawatha*. Pictures by Susan Jeffers. New York: Dial Books for Young Readers, 1983

 Computer and printer

 Paper

 Crayons

 Pencil

 Stapler and staples

 Teacher-made example book

 Optional: Wildlife magazines or books

Materials Preparation

1. Use a computer and printer with a program such as "Print Shop" (Broderbund Software, Inc., 1985) to make the pages for a book. (If a computer is unavailable, use a typewriter.)

   a. The student will type a title page "Hiawatha's Brothers" by _____ _____ .

   b. The student will type the name of an animal that was in the *Hiawatha* book, such as deer, moose, squirrel, rabbit, beaver, bear, on each page. He or she will assemble the pages into a book, then illustrate it. The student may refer to the pictures in the Hiawatha book, wildlife books, or wildlife magazines.

   c. You will need to determine the number of pages and the way to assemble the book. Optional: older students could arrange the animal pages in alphabetical order.

Directions for File Folder Activities

Activity 1

The student will type the words on the pages and make a book per your directions.

Activity 2

The student will illustrate the pages. He or she may wish to visit another classroom to read the completed book. (See "Enjoying Language Arts" for more details.)

Takeoff

1. Students may enjoy learning about the habitats of "Hiawatha's Brothers." They could draw pictures or make a class mural depicting the animals in their habitats.

2. The students may create stationery with animal headings on the computer also.

Hiawatha

by Henry Wadsworth Longfellow

1 Type the words on the pages.

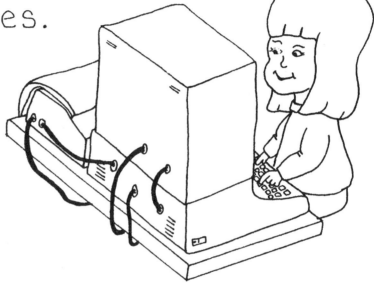

2 Draw the animal pictures in your book.

Hiawatha
File Folder Directions

TEACHER'S DIRECTIONS FOR *THE BAKER'S DOZEN* CENTER

Skills Reading, math, creating, art, fine-motor coordination

Materials Needed

> Book: Forest, Heather, *The Baker's Dozen,* Orlando, FL: Harcourt Brace Jovanovich, 1988
>
> Copies of Student Activity Page (see page 208)
>
> Six transparent plastic containers with lids, such as small peanut butter jars
>
> A collection of six kinds of objects (different sizes and shapes) such as beans, cotton balls, keys, shells, pasta, nuts, buttons, erasers, small pine cones
>
> An assortment of small cookie cutters (less than 2″ in size)
>
> Rolling pin
>
> Pencil
>
> Teacher-made clay
>
> One plastic bag (self-sealing) per student

Materials Preparation

1. Read the book *The Baker's Dozen* aloud to the class, emphasizing that a baker's dozen means thirteen.

2. Provide six transparent plastic containers with lids and six different sets of objects (one kind per container) for students to count. Some ideas are beans, keys, nuts, buttons, erasers, small pine cones.

Fill two containers with thirteen objects, two containers with less than thirteen objects, and two containers with more than thirteen objects. (You may wish to have the class practice estimating the objects in one of the containers prior to beginning this center.)

3. Make clay in a quantity sufficient for your class (each student will make thirteen cookies) using the following recipe or your own favorite.

> Ingredients:
>
> 1 cup salt
>
> 1 cup hot water
>
> ½ cup cold water
>
> 1 cup cornstarch

> Directions:
>
> a. Mix the salt and hot water in a pan and bring to boiling point.
>
> b. Stir the cold water into the cornstarch.

c. Add the cornstarch mixture to the boiling water. Stir vigorously to prevent lumps.

d. Cook over low heat, stirring constantly, until the mixture is like stiff pie dough. You may add food coloring if desired.

e. Remove from heat and turn out onto a breadboard to cool.

f. As soon as the mixture is cool enough to handle, knead until smooth and pliable.

This makes about 3 cups of clay. Cookies or objects will dry and harden. When dry, it can be painted. Divide the clay into self-sealing plastic bags (one per student). The clay will keep for a long period of time without refrigeration.

4. Demonstrate techniques for rolling out dough with a rolling pin, using a cookie cutter to make a baker's dozen of cookies, and putting them into the plastic bag (reuse the original self-sealing clay plastic bag) to take home. The cookies may be dried at home.

Directions for File Folder Activities

Activity 1

The student will estimate the number of objects in each of the six containers. He or she will record his or her guess on the Student Activity Page. Then the student will count the number of objects in the containers and record the number.

Activity 2

The student will make a baker's dozen of cookies per your directions. He or she will put the cookies in a plastic bag to take them home.

Takeoff

1. Make a class bread-loaf shape book. Draw an outline of a loaf of bread on paper. Duplicate a page for each student. The student will draw a baker's dozen of food which could be found in a bakery, for example, cookies, pretzels, cupcakes, doughnuts, and so on. Compile the pages into a class book. Students may share the book at home, as described in "Enjoying Language Arts."

2. Your class may wish to do other estimation activities. You could reuse the jars from the center for a variety of objects.

The Baker's Dozen

Retold by Heather Forest

1 Guess, then count the objects.

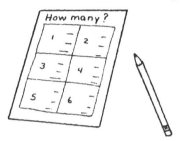

2 Make a Baker's Dozen of cookies.

How many?

name _____

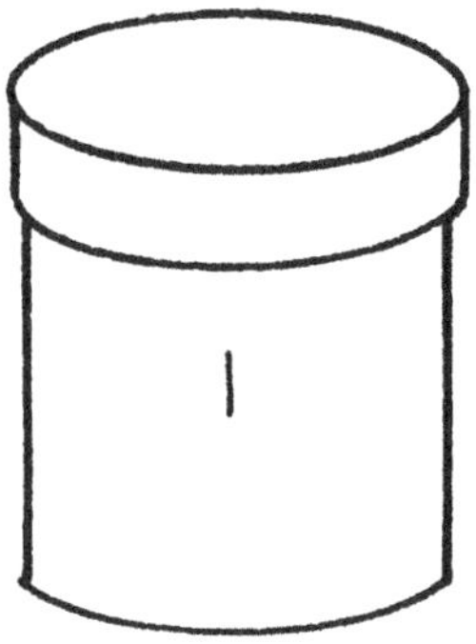

guess _____

count _____

1

Baker's Dozen? _____

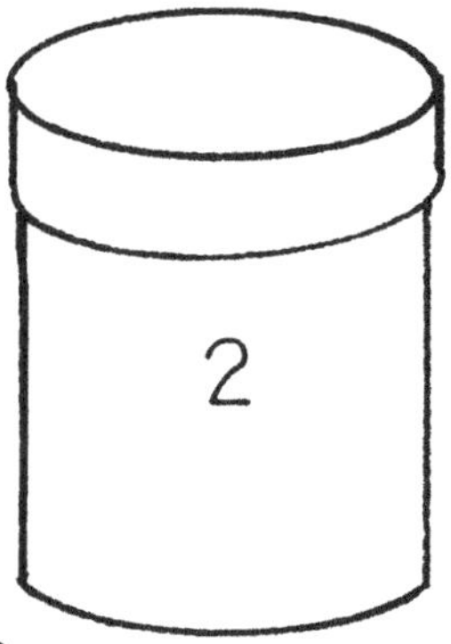

guess _____

count _____

2

Baker's Dozen? _____

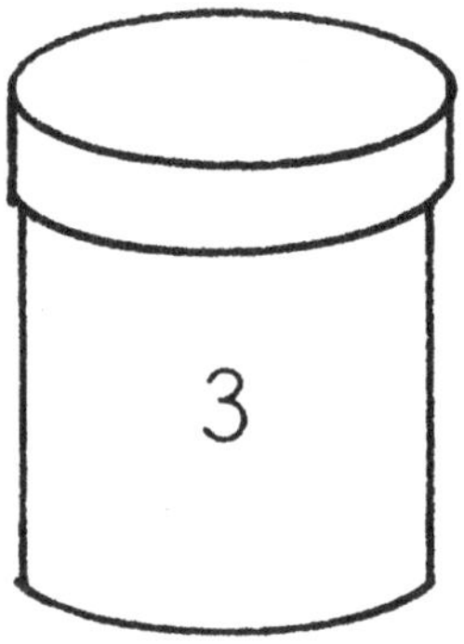

guess _____

count _____

3

Baker's Dozen? _____

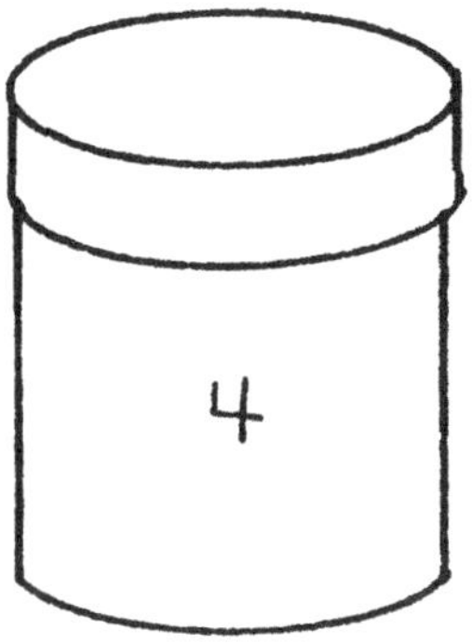

guess _____

count _____

4

Baker's Dozen? _____

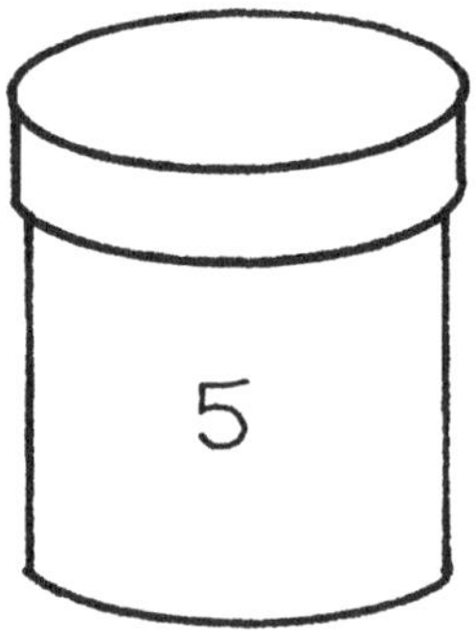

guess _____

count _____

5

Baker's Dozen? _____

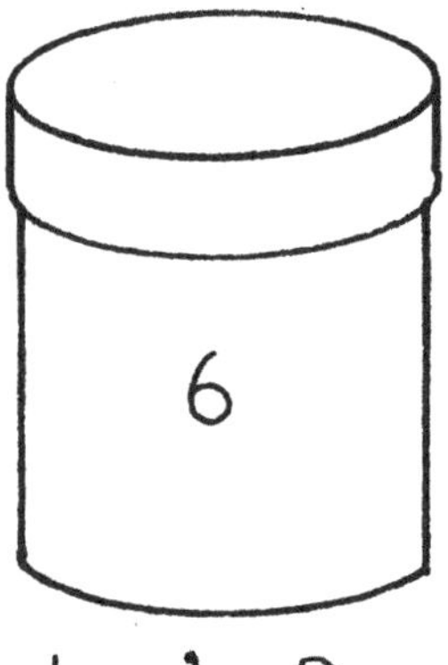

guess _____

count _____

6

Baker's Dozen? _____

The Baker's Dozen
Student Activity Page

American Tall Tales and Legends Enrichment Activities

TEACHER'S DIRECTIONS FOR "AMERICAN TALL TALES AND LEGENDS" ENRICHMENT ACTIVITIES

"American Tall Tales and Legends" Group Activity

As a culminating activity to the American Tall Tales and Legends Language Arts unit, schedule an American Tall Tales and Legends Celebration. The following are suggested activities you may want to do:

1. Plan to have a Paul Bunyan and His Friends Breakfast. Organize parents to bring in electric griddles or frying pans and the pancake ingredients. The parents can assist small groups of students in mixing, making, serving, and eating pancakes.

2. As a Johnny Appleseed spinoff, you may want to make applesauce or apple salad with parental help.

3. Divide the students into pairs to review Spelling words by playing the Casey Jones Spelling Race game.

4. Share the "American Tall Tales and Legends" Research Activity stories. Encourage family members to attend and perhaps relate other family legends.

5. Open the classroom "mailbox" and give the students the opportunity to read the letters they wrote to the parents of American tall tales characters (see the creative writing assignment, page 212).

6. Encourage parents to visit your classroom dressed as one of their favoriate American tall tales characters. They may read or retell their story about the characters to small groups of students. Rotate the groups of students to the parents, enabling them to hear all the stories. The parents would tell the story to as many groups as you have designated. (To see how to recruit parent help, refer to "Enjoying Language Arts.")

7. Create puppet shows. Divide the class into small groups to make puppets and retell their favorite American tall tale or legend. (You may want to have an adult aide per group if the entire class works on puppets at the same time.) Invite parents to attend the puppet shows. Your students may wish to perform puppet shows for another class, too, as described in the last section of this book.

8. Make bookmarks to give to the people who read to the students for the "American Tall Tales and Legends" Read-at-Home Activity.

9. As a takeoff to *The Baker's Dozen* center, you may wish to do a variety of math estimation activities.

10. Videotape the American Tall Tales and Legends Celebration activities and send the tape home with the students. (See the last section of this book for details.)

"American Tall Tales and Legends" Read-at-Home Activity

Encourage parents, grandparents, other family members, and friends to read aloud American tall tales and legends to the children. They should record the titles, reader's names, dates read, and the child's comments on the "American Tall Tales and Legends" Read-at-Home Activity Page.

"American Tall Tales and Legends" Read-at-Home Award

When the students return the signed "American Tall Tales and Legends" Read-at-Home Activity Page, determine the total number of persons listed as "readers" for your class. Duplicate the total number of awards needed for your class on colored paper. The students will give awards to each of the people listed as readers. (The student will write the reader's name as well as his or her own name on the award. The student may wish to color the pictures on the award.)

"American Tall Tales and Legends" Spelling Activity

1. You may want to read aloud a book about Casey Jones, such as *Casey Jones Drives an Ice Cream Train* by Adele Deleeuw (Champaing, IL: Garrard Publishing Co., 1971), *Casey Jones* by Jan Gleiter and Kathleen Thompson (Milwaukee, WI: Raintree Publishers, 1987), and *Casey Jones* by Carol B. York (Mahwah, NY: Troll Associates, 1980) prior to using this page.

2. Duplicate the Casey Jones Spelling Activity Pages 1 and 2 onto heavy paper.

3. The student will color the pictures and the railroad track on the Casey Jones Spelling Activity Page 1. He or she will use the page as a gameboard.

4. The student will write his or her spelling words on the Casey Jones Spelling Activity Page 2 (one word per card) and cut out the cards.

5. The student will use his or her Casey Jones spelling race gameboard, spelling cards, a die, and two markers (such as checkers) to play the game with a friend. The players place their markers at the "Depot," and each player draws a spelling card for the opponent and reads the word aloud. If the opponent spells the word correctly, he or she throws the die and advances the appropriate number of spaces on the railroad track. (If the opponent spells the word incorrectly, he or she does not throw the die.) The players take turns drawing the spelling cards. The player who reaches the Finish first is the winner.

"American Tall Tales and Legends" Creative Writing Activity

Discuss the American tall tales and legends books used at the centers and other similar books that are familiar to your class. You may want to list the characters in the books on chart paper. Review the outstanding characteristics of the people with your class.

Creative writing assignment. Pretend you are the teacher of one of the tall-tale characters when he or she was your age. Write a letter to the parent of this character on the Creative Writing Activity Page. (Younger students may dictate the letter to an aide.) You may illustrate the letter on the back of the page. For example: "Dear Mrs. Van Winkle, please see that your child, Rip, gets more sleep at night. He needs to stay awake in my class. His snoring is bothering the other students. Thank you for your help. Sincerely, _____."

You may want to have the students put their letters in envelopes and place them in a classroom mailbox. Open the mailbox at a later date, such as the group activity day, and let the students share their letters. You may also want to publish the letters in a school newspaper or class traveling book, as described in "Enjoying Language Arts."

"American Tall Tales and Legends" Research Activity

Read *The Black Snowman* by Phil Mendez (New York: Scholastic, 1989) to your students. Discuss with them the things they know about their grandparents and other ancestors. Next, read aloud *Knots on a Counting Rope* by Bill Martin, Jr., and John Archambault (New York: Henry Holt and Co., 1987). Discuss the way the counting rope helped the boy memorize his legend.

Explain the research project. The student will write a story about him- or herself or an ancestor with the help of his or her family on the Research Activity Page. The student will tie a knot in a counting rope each time he or she tells the story.

Send the Legends Old and New Letter, the Research Activity page, and a 12″ piece of twine home with each student. You may then want to have the stories and the ropes returned on the group activity day. The students could share their stories.

"American Tall Tales and Legends" Summary Page

The student will refer to the books in this section or to other resources to determine the location(s) where each legend took place in the United States. He or she will draw an appropriate symbol for each legend's location(s) on the U.S. map on the Summary Page. (Prior to duplicating the Summary page, you will need to make a legend symbol color or shape key in the box. Some ideas are a lasso for *Pecos Bill,* an apple for *Johnny Appleseed,* a hammer for *John Henry,* a beard for *Rip Van Winkle,* a cookie for *The Baker's Dozen,* and so on.)

"American Tall Tales and Legends"
Read-at-Home Activity Page

Return by _____

Date _____

Dear Parent,

    "American Tall Tales and Legends" is the theme of our language arts learning centers. Included are Paul Bunyan, Johnny Appleseed, Rip Van Winkle, Pecos Bill, John Henry, and others.

    Remember when you first heard these stories? Please help your child's love of reading grow by retelling these stories. Go with your child to the library and select some American tall tales and legends. Encourage your child's grandparents, other family members, and friends to read aloud the stories to your child. I am sure they will enjoy sharing some of their favorite tall tales and legends.

    Please have the reader record the title, reader's name, dates read, and the child's comments on the attached "American Tall Tales and Legends" Read-at-Home Activity Page. Return the page on _____ . A surprise award will be given upon receipt of the signed and completed page.

    Thank you and all the readers for helping your child discover the joy of listening to tales from the past.

Sincerely,

_____

Your child's teacher

Legend or Tall Tale read:	Reader's name:	Date(s) read:	Child's comments:

Please return this page to school on _____.

_____
parent signature

_____
student's name

"American Tall Tales and Legends"
Read-at-Home Activity Page

Read At Home

HURRAH!
Read At Home

Dear _____,

Thank you for reading
American Tall Tales and Legends.

_____

"American Tall Tales and Legends"
Read-at-Home Award

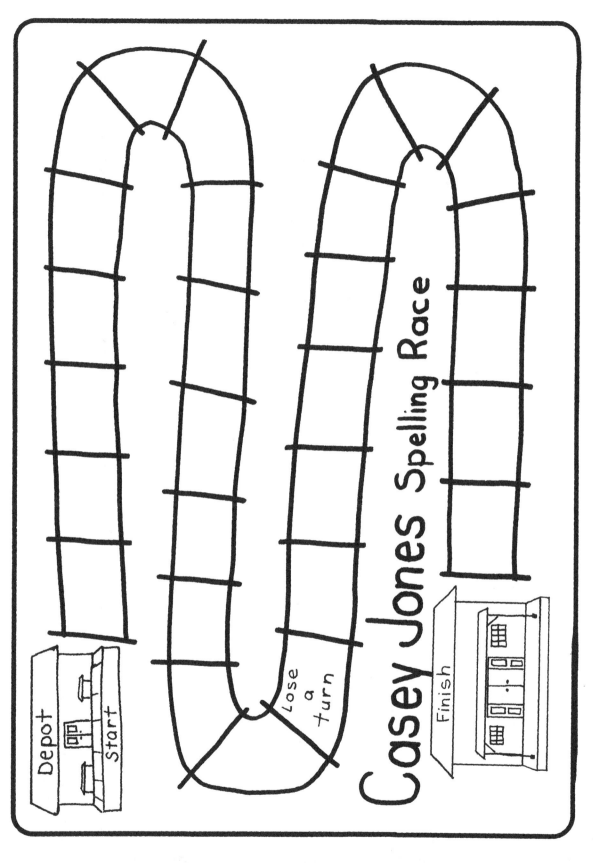

Depot

Start

Lose a turn

Casey Jones Spelling Race

Finish

"American Tall Tales and Legends"
Spelling Activity Page 2

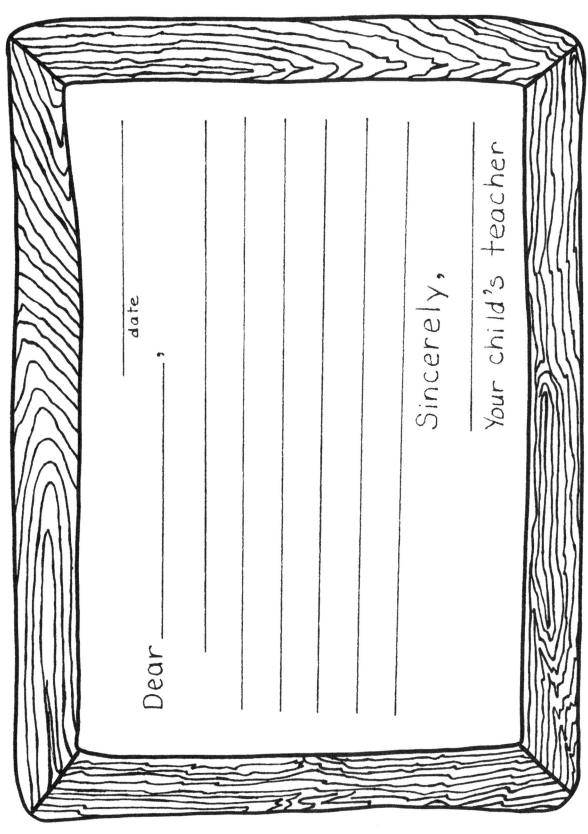

Dear _____ ,

_____
date

Sincerely,

_____
Your child's teacher

Legends Old and New

Date _____

Dear Parent,

    As you know, our current language arts learning centers feature characters from American tall tales. These stories, in most cases, were originally passed on from one generation to another by the oral tradition rather than written. Some of the characters we have met were real, but their actions have made them "legendary" as people have continued to retell their stories.

    I have just finished reading two books to our class. *The Black Snowman* by Phil Mendez gave us the message that it is important for us to remember that our ancestors gave us a heritage. We should draw strength and courage from that heritage by being aware of their brave actions and ways of life.

    The other book was *Knots on a Counting Rope* by Bill Martin, Jr., and John Archambault. The book is about a little boy who learns to tell the story of his own childhood by carefully retelling it with the help of his grandfather. Each time the story was repeated, the boy tied a knot in his "counting rope." When the rope became full of knots, the boy knew the story from memory.

    Please help your child with this research project by telling him or her a story about himself, herself, yourself, a grandparent, or other relative. You may wish to tell a story about an old photograph or special object. Please write the story on the attached page or help your child write it. Encourage your child to tell the story several times. Each time he or she tells the story from memory, a knot may be tied in the counting rope attached to this note.

    Please return the story and rope to school on _____ . If the story is about a special object, please use your own discretion about sending it to school (you may prefer to send a photograph of it instead). Your child may wish to make a cover for this report.

    Thank you for your help with this project.

Sincerely,

_____
Your child's teacher

"American Tall Tales and Legends"
Research Activity Page

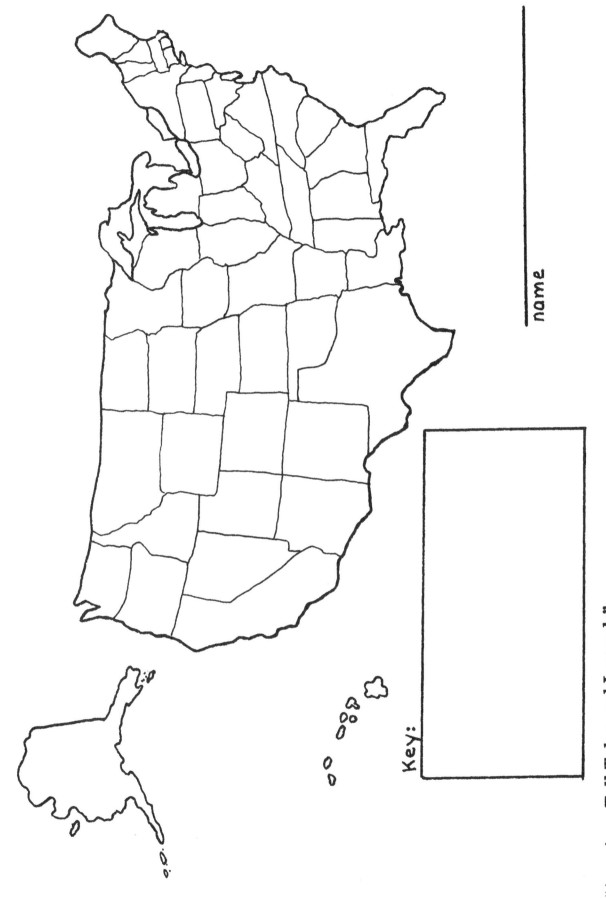

name

Key:

"American Tall Tales and Legends"
Summary Page

Bibliography

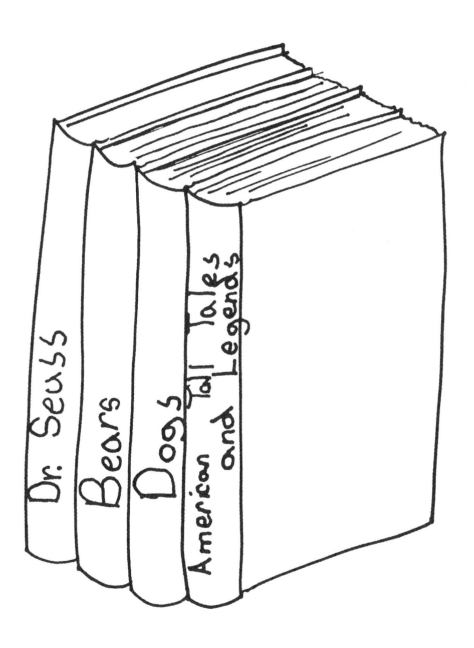

"DR. SEUSS AND HIS FRIENDS" BIBLIOGRAPHY

LE SIEG, THEO., *In a People House*. New York: Random House, 1972.

LE SIEG, THEO., *Ten Apples up on Top*. New York: Random House, 1961.

LE SIEG, THEO., *Wacky Wednesday*. New York: Random House, 1974.

SEUSS, DR., *The Cat in the Hat*. New York: Random House, 1957.

SEUSS, DR., *The Cat in the Hat Comes Back*. New York: Random House, 1958.

SEUSS, DR., *Dr. Seuss's A B C*. New York: Random House, 1963.

SEUSS, DR., *The 500 Hats of Bartholomew Cubbins*. New York: Vanguard Press, 1938.

SEUSS, DR., *Fox in Socks*. New York: Random House, 1965.

SEUSS, DR., *Green Eggs and Ham*. New York: Random House, 1960.

SEUSS, DR., *The Lorax*. New York: Random House, 1971.

SEUSS, DR., *McElligot's Pool*. New York: Random House, 1947.

SEUSS, DR., *Oh, Say Can You Say?* New York: Random House, 1979.

"BEARS" BIBLIOGRAPHY

ALEXANDER, MARTHA, *We're in Trouble, Blackboard Bear*. New York: Dial Press, 1980.

BERENSTAIN, STAN AND JAN, *The Bear's Picnic*. New York: Random House, 1966.

BERENSTAIN, STAN AND JAN, *The Bike Lesson*. New York: Random House, 1964.

BERENSTAIN, STAN AND JAN, *Too Much T.V.* New York: Random House, 1984.

CARLSTROM, NANCY WHITE, *Jesse Bear, What Will You Wear?* New York: Macmillan, 1986.

CONWAY, JUDITH, *More Magic Tricks*. Mahwah, NJ: Troll Associates, 1987.

DELTON, JUDY, *Bear and Duck on the Run*. Niles, IL: Albert Whitman and Co., 1984.

DELTON, JUDY, *Brimhall Turns to Magic*. New York: William Morrow and Co., 1979.

FREEMAN, DON, *Corduroy*. New York: Viking Press, 1968.

FREEMAN, DON, *A Pocket for Corduroy,* New York: Viking Press, 1978.

GRETZ, SUSANNA, AND ALISON SAGE, *Teddy Bears Cure a Cold*. New York: Scholastic, 1984.

HOBAN, LILLIAN, *Arthur's Honey Bear*. New York: Harper and Row, 1974.

ISENBERG, BARBARA, AND MARJORIE JAFFE, *Albert the Running Bear's Exercise Book*. New York: Clarion Books, 1984.

ISENBERG, BARBARA, AND SUSAN WOLF, *Albert the Running Bear Gets the Jitters*. New York: Clarion Books, 1987.

KENNEDY, JIMMY, *The Teddy Bear's Picnic*. New York: Bedrick/Blackie, 1987.

LORD, SUZANNE, *Grin and Bear It, The Teddy Bear Joke Book*. New York: Parachute Press, 1986.

MARTIN, BILL, JR., *Brown Bear, Brown Bear, What Do You See?* New York: Holt, Rinehart and Winston, 1970.

McCLOSKEY, ROBERT, *Blueberries for Sal*. New York: Viking Press, 1948.

McLEOD, EMILIE WARREN, *The Bear's Bicycle*. Boston: Little, Brown, 1975.

McPHAIL, DAVID, *Fix-It*. New York: E. P. Dutton, 1984.

MINARIK, ELSE HOLMELUND, *Little Bear*. New York: Harper and Row, 1974.

SHARMAT, MARJORIE WEINMAN, *I'm Terrific*. New York: Holiday House, 1977.

SIVULICH, SANDRA STRONER. *I'm Going on a Bear Hunt*. New York: E. P. Dutton, 1973.

WABER, BERNARD, *Ira Sleeps Over*. Boston: Houghton-Mifflin Co., 1972.

WYLER, ROSE, AND GERALD AMES, *Funny Magic*. New York: Parents' Magazine Press, 1972.

WYLER, ROSE, AND GERALD AMES, *Magic Secrets*. New York: Bantam Doubleday Dell, 1990.

YEOMAN, JOHN, *The Bear's Picnic*. New York: Macmillan, 1970.

"DOGS" BIBLIOGRAPHY

BRIDWELL, NORMAN, *Clifford Takes a Trip*. New York: Scholastic, 1966.

GACKENBACH, DICK, *Dog for a Day*. New York: Clarion Books, 1987.

GRIFFITH, HELEN M., *Mine Will, Said John*. New York: Greenwillow Books, 1980.

KELLOGG, STEVEN, *Tallyho, Pinkerton!* New York: Dial Press, 1982.

O'NEILL, CATHERINE, *Mrs. Dunphy's Dog*. New York: Viking Penguin, 1987.

PEET, BILL, *The Whingdingdilly*. Boston: Houghton-Mifflin, 1970.

SCHULZ, CHARLES M., *Snoopy*. New York: Holt, Rinehart and Winston, 1958.

SELSAM, MILLICENT, AND JOYCE HUNT, *Keep Looking!* New York: Macmillan, 1989.

WILDSMITH, BRIAN, *Give a Dog a Bone*. New York: Pantheon Books, 1985.

ZION, GENE, *No Roses for Harry*. New York: Harper and Row, 1958.

"AMERICAN TALL TALES AND LEGENDS" BIBLIOGRAPHY

Rip Van Winkle

GIPSON, MORRELL, *Rip Van Winkle.* Garden City, NY: Doubleday, 1987.
LOCKER, THOMAS, *Rip Van Winkle.* New York: Dial Books, 1988.
YORK, CAROL BEACH, *Washington Irving's Rip Van Winkle.* Mahway, NJ: Troll Associates, 1980.

The Legend of the Indian Paintbrush

DE PAOLA, TOMIE, *The Legend of the Indian Paintbrush.* New York: G. P. Putnam's Sons, 1988.

John Henry

KEATS, EZRA JACK, *John Henry.* New York: Knopf, 1987.
NADEN, C. J., *John Henry.* Mahwah, NJ: Troll Associates, 1980.

Pecos Bill

DEWEY, ARIANE, *Pecos Bill.* New York: Greenwillow Books, 1983.
KELLOGG, STEVEN, *Pecos Bill.* New York: William Morrow, 1986.

Johnny Appleseed

ANDERSON, J. I., *I Can Read About Johnny Appleseed.* Mahwah, NJ: Troll Associates, 1977.
ANDERSON, LA VERE, *Johnny Appleseed.* Champaign, IL: Garrard, 1974.
KELLOGG, STEVEN, *Johnny Appleseed.* New York: William Morrow and Co., 1988.

Paul Bunyan

DOLAN, ELLEN M., AND JANET L., BOLINSKE, *Paul Bunyan.* St. Louis, MO: Milliken, 1987.
KELLOGG, STEVEN, *Paul Bunyan.* New York: William Morrow and Co., 1984.
SYMAN, NANCI A., *Paul Bunyan.* Mahwah, NJ: Troll Associates, 1980.

Hiawatha

LONGFELLOW, HENRY WADSWORTH, *Hiawatha.* Pictures by Susan Jeffers. New York: Dial Books for Young Readers, 1983.

The Baker's Dozen

FOREST, HEATHER, *The Baker's Dozen.* Orlando, FL: Harcourt Brace Jovanovich, 1988.

Additional Books in This Chapter

DELEEUW, ADELE, *Casey Jones Drives an Ice Cream Train.* Champaign, IL: Garrard, 1971.

GLEITER, JAN, AND KATHLEEN THOMPSON, *Casey Jones.* Milwaukee, WI: Raintree, 1987.

HOFSINDE, ROBERT, *Indian Sign Language.* New York: William Morrow & Co., 1956.

HUNT, W. BEN, *Indian and Camp Handicraft.* New York: The Bruce Publishing Co., 1938.

HUNT, W. BEN, *The Complete Book of Indian Crafts Lore.* New York: Golden Press, 1954.

MARTIN, BILL, JR., AND JOHN ARCHAMBAULT, *Knots on a Counting Rope.* New York: Henry Holt and Co., 1987.

MENDEZ, PHIL, *The Black Snowman.* New York: Scholastic, 1989.

Wolf Cub Scout Book. Irving, TX: Boy Scouts of America, 1986.

YORK, CAROL B., *Casey Jones.* Mahwah, NJ: Troll Associates, 1980.

Enjoying Language Arts

The secret of successfully turning a child on to literature is to expose the child to as much literature as possible. The child who is provided with many language opportunities will also build a broader vocabulary, expand his or her general knowledge, and gain greater facility in speaking and writing. How can teachers turn children on to reading when they are competing with television, which has masterfully produced child-oriented programs? The attraction to television screens is further enhanced by the challenge of video games and by parents who are willing to allow their children to spend excessive amounts of time in front of the screen.

Our challenge as teachers is to make language encounters fun. The pursuit of reading will then become an attractive alternative to television and video games. Parents must also become aware of their responsibilities in guiding their children toward the alternatives that will lead the children to expand their imagination and creativity.

This section shows parents their role in supporting their child's growth in language skills. The activities your students complete at school and share at home are accompanied by reproducible explanatory notes. The enjoyable language arts experiences your students make can also be shared with their peers at school. Reinforcement of their language skills can then take place.

Wonderful language arts programs can become more than the two hands of a teacher can manage. This chapter gives you ideas about recruiting willing parents and other community members to volunteer time to help you at home or at school.

REINFORCEMENT DURING SCHOOL

An important part of any language arts program is to provide many opportunities for the child to reread the story or book he or she has written. To achieve this purpose at school, you may want to arrange for the child to visit another classroom to read to another sibling or friend. The "In-School Note—Reading" may be used to introduce this child to the teacher of that room. Children may also enjoy reading to the principal or other support staff.

When your students produce a play, skit, puppet show, rap, poem, and so on, they may enjoy sharing it with others. The "In-School Note—Production" can quickly be filled out for another teacher so arrangements can be made to share the production.

REINFORCEMENT OF SKILLS AT HOME

Reinforcement of language arts in the home of the child not only strengthens the skills of the student, but can provide meaningful language encounters for the child and his or her parent. The letter "Helping Your Child at Home With Reading" will help parents understand their role in helping their child with reading. You may want to send it home in the fall. The letter will also encourage parents to anticipate receiving special reading activities that will be sent home.

Dear _____,

_____ has just written a story! He/She would like to read it to _____.

Thank you!

_____
teacher's name

☐ The story was read.   ☐ This is not a good time. Come back at _____ _____.

Dear _____,

Our class has written a story! A member of my class, _____, would like to read it to _____, in your class.

Thank you for your time!

_____
teacher's name

☐ The story was read.   ☐ This is not a good time. Come back at _____ _____.

Language Arts Reinforcement
In-School Note—Reading

Now Showing:

Dear _____,

    Members of my class would like to
perform a ☐ play ☐ puppet show ☐ rap ☐_____
for your students. It would take about____ minutes.
Location:_____.
What time on _____ would be convenient?
                    (day of week?)
How about _____ or _____? Circle one
or give an alternative time. _____
                    Thank you!
                    _____

Language Arts Reinforcement
In-School Note—Production

Helping Your Child at Home with Reading

September _____

Dear Parent,

I am often asked by parents the following question: "How can I help my child become a better reader?" There are many answers to this important question. Perhaps these guidelines will help both you and your child during the following year.

One responsibility you must demonstrate to your young reader is to show how important reading is to you. Set a good example by reading newspapers, magazines, or books in front of your child. Make good use of the public library to help your child also develop the interest and love for books. As your child learns to read, don't stop the enjoyable event of reading aloud. You can still increase the speaking vocabulary of your child by exposing him or her to new stories. Do not despair if your child should happen to ask for the same story to be read over and over, because his or her love of books has begun already!

Another responsibility is to show an interest in your child's new skill of reading. Continue to praise your child for any small or large accomplishment. Find time to review school work with him or her. Throughout the school year, I will send home special fun activities or books for you to share with your child. Most of them are created to encourage your child to devote more time to reading at home in an enjoyable and meaningful way.

Finally, effective growth in reading will require you to provide the basic physical, social, emotional, and language needs for your child. Make sure your child gets adequate rest and food. In addition, provide vision and hearing screening. Language needs can be met by giving your child as many experiences as possible and explaining these experiences to the child. Usually, the more experiences your child has, the better reader he or she will become.

You are the first teacher your child had and your role continues as a teacher—even now that your child has entered school. You are a key factor in how well your child will do in school. With your support and your child's efforts, the three of us will work together to help your child enjoy reading.

Sincerely,

_____
Your child's teacher

REINFORCEMENT ACTIVITIES FOR THE HOME

Traveling books, videos, animals, scrapbooks, storybags, and take-home puppet shows are all devices that extend the activities you do at school back to the home. The notes that go home with each of these activities further communicate with the home how the activities should be used. You will be able to use some of the projects your class and individual students create from the learning centers as take-home activities.

Traveling Books

A traveling book is a book written by members of your class. It travels with one of the authors to the person(s), such as family members, with whom the child wishes to share it. The book is shared overnight and returned to school so that its other coauthors may have turns sharing it with their families as well.

In order that parents or other family members will know the book should be returned promptly, you should attach the "Note to Parents" to the book. As parents sign the log, it is not difficult to determine which students need a turn next. Students will enjoy reading the positive comments about their books, too. NOTE: Be sure to provide a tote bag for the book to travel in!

Date _____

Dear Parent,

    Our class has compiled a book called _____ . Your child wanted to share it with you tonight. Please return it to school tomorrow or the next school day so other students may share it with their families soon. Thank you for taking the time to listen to your child.
    Please sign the log so I know the book was read.

Sincerely,

_____

Your child's teacher

Traveling Book
Note to Parents

Thank you for taking the time to go over this "Traveling Book" with your child. Our class <u>loves</u> to read your comments. Please print a comment on the lines below and sign your name.
Thank you!

_____

_____

_____

_____

_____

_____

_____

_____

_____

_____

_____

_____

_____

_____

_____

_____

_____

_____

Traveling Book
Parent Log

Thank you for taking the time to go over this "Traveling Book" with your child. Our class enjoys seeing how y<u>ou</u> would have finished a page. There are blank pages which follow this page. You and any other family members may create your own page. Sign your name(s) and return the book to school promptly!

Thank you!

_____

(Title of Book)

_____

(Date Written)

TABLE OF CONTENTS

Name of person who made the page: Page Number:

_____ . . . . _____

_____ . . . . _____

_____ . . . . _____

_____ . . . . _____

_____ . . . . _____

_____ . . . . _____

_____ . . . . _____

_____ . . . . _____

_____ . . . . _____

_____ . . . . _____

_____ . . . . _____

_____ . . . . _____

_____ . . . . _____

_____ . . . . _____

_____ . . . . _____

_____ . . . . _____

_____ . . . . _____

_____ . . . . _____

_____ . . . . _____

_____ . . . . _____

Traveling Book
Table of Contents

If the book has been of the "finish-the-sentence" type, family members may want to add their own pages. Put blank pages at the end of the book for them as well, as explained in the "Add-a-Page" note.

Sometimes your children may write a spinoff of another author's book. If possible, you may want to include the original book that was read to the children and from which the traveling book evolved.

Traveling book checkout: You will probably want to keep track of the books so that you know when a book is overdue. A list for each traveling book with the name of the latest checkout at the bottom works well. When the book is returned, the student's name is crossed out. A class librarian may be selected to help maintain the records.

Another way is to have a card with each child's name in a box. When a child takes home the book, he or she hangs the card so that you know that particular child has a book at home. When the book is returned to school, the child puts his or her card back into the box.

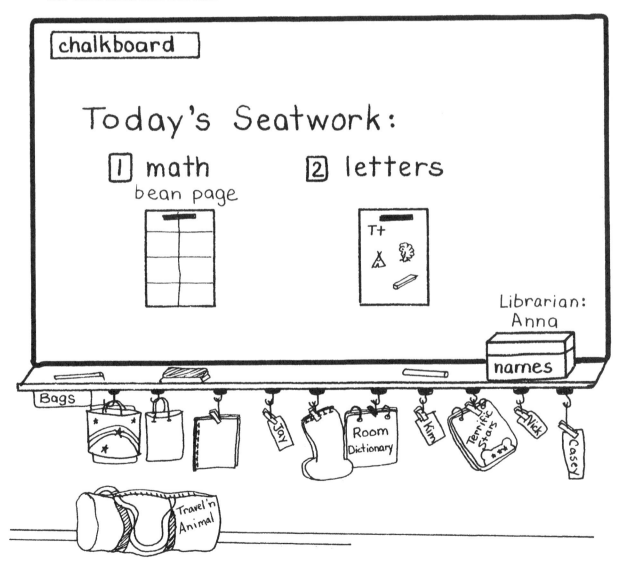

Displaying traveling books: There are several ways to display the class books so that all students can share. See the illustration above as well as the one on page 239 for ideas that could work for your classroom.

Making traveling books more durable: Traveling books often take a great deal of abuse in their travels! Here are some hints to minimize wear and tear:

1. Make covers for the book of heavy oaktag or posterboard.

2. Laminate the covers and all the pages, if possible. Use clear, self-stick vinyl.

3. Bind the pages with heavy-duty staples, plastic chicken bands (available from farm supply stores and toy stores, where they are called Chinese jacks), metal rings, or plastic binding done with a plastic-binding machine. Plastic garbage ties are another inexpensive way of fastening the pages together into a book. Put a piece of tape on the back of each page prior to punching holes in it to reinforce the page and prevent it from tearing out of the book.

4. Provide plastic, canvas, or recycled shopping bags for the books to travel in to and from school. Perhaps you would be able to recruit a parent who sews who can make several bags for this purpose. Directions for making fabric tote bags are given under the section entitled Recruiting Help.

Traveling Videos

Videotape plays, puppet shows, favorite books, takeoff activities, group activities, special occasions, and so on, with the school video camera. If possible, you might have a different tape of each set of learning centers and its related activities. Another way is to keep a cumulative record of your class year by continually adding to the tape.

Traveling videos provide parents and family members with a unique opportunity to view their child's education in action. Some working parents and extended family members are unable to visit their child's classroom, but can do so when supplied with a videotape. With the growing popularity of VCRs, more families have one in their homes or in the home of someone they know. The traveling videos can also be shown at an Open House to parents who do not own a VCR.

If possible, enlist the help of one or two parents who are willing to be your camerapeople. Allow the students the opportunity to get used to being in front of a camera before an "official" taping session begins. Their behavior will be more predictable and natural when they are used to being videotaped.

Some parents may want to copy the tape. You may have a trained parent or school library person copy the tape(s) if your school has the necessary equipment. Do this at the end of the school year for any parents willing to provide a blank tape.

The traveling video's Note to Parents can be put in an envelope taped to the sturdy case that contains the tape. Provide a bag for the tape to travel in.

Traveling Animals

Your class may enjoy adopting a stuffed animal. The purpose of this ongoing activity is to encourage creativity and language skills.

Select a plush stuffed animal and a duffle bag in which the animal will comfortably fit. You may want to choose an animal that relates to a unit in this book. As a group, you might name the animal. Also provide a spiral-bound notebook with lined paper for the animal's daily journal.

Each night, a different student takes the animal home in the bag. The student includes the animal in his or her home routine as if the animal were an invited friend. The animal's activities are written down in the journal by the student or dictated by the student to a parent. You might take the animal home the first night and write the first entry to set an example for what you expect to have written each night.

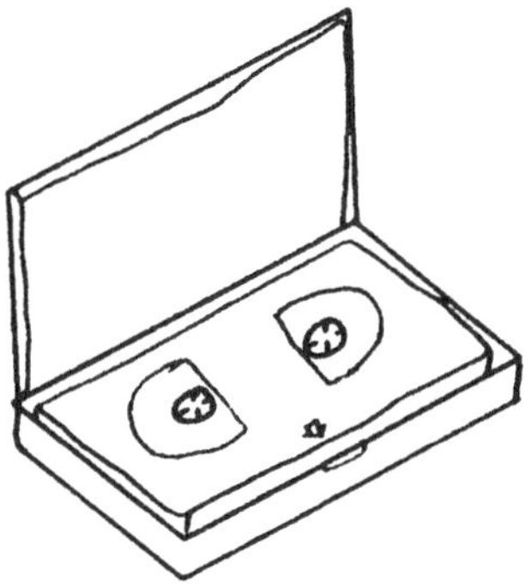

Dear Parent,

Our class has compiled a videotape of _____
_____ . Your child wants to share it with
you tonight. Please return it to school tomorrow or the
next school day so that other students can share the tape
with their families soon.

Please see that this tape is not subjected to extreme
heat or cold. Do not leave the tape in the sun. This could
permanently damage or erase our tape and ruin the fun
for others.

Please sign the log below so I know the tape was
viewed. When more lines are needed for the log, please use
the back of this sheet.

Sincerely,

_____

Your child's teacher

**Traveling Video
Note to Parent**

242

The traveling animal's "Note to Parents" is an example of one that should be laminated and attached to the animal's journal. You may want to keep a copy handy in the event the original is misplaced.

Traveling Puppet Shows

Your students will have fun thinking of and creating puppets for known stories or for original stories. Provide a bag for the puppets, as well as a parent comment sheet and the traveling puppet show's Note to Parents.

Traveling Storybags

Let your students create their own stories using drawn characters backed with flannel and a flannelboard. Their storytelling can be brought home in a bag along with the traveling storybag's Note to Parents and a comment sheet.

Dear Parent,

   My name is _____ . I belong to the children in _____'s
class. Today, I am happy to come home with your child for the evening. As you can tell when
you read my journal with your child, I have had many adventures with other members
of _____'s class. Please write down the things I did with your child. Make
sure I return to school tomorrow morning in my bag with my journal because I am trying to
have a perfect attendance record! Thank you.

Sincerely,

_____

Name of animal

You may insert a photograph of your Traveling Animal or have a student draw one here !

Traveling Animal
Note to Parent

Dear Parent,

    In this bag is a story ready to be told titled: _____ . Please listen to your child tell the story using the _____ puppets.
_{number}
Family members are welcome to take parts the second time through the play. Additions, variations or surprise endings are always fun too! This activity should promote the growth of your child's oral language.

    Thank you for taking time to make this activity a special one for your child!

    Return the bag and contents tomorrow.

        Sincerely,

Traveling Puppet Show
Note to Parent

Dear Parent,

In this bag is a story ready to be told titled:_____.
Please listen to your child tell the story using the _____ props with the flannel board.

number

This activity should promote the growth of your child's oral language.

Thank you for taking the time to make this activity a special one for your child!

Return the bag and its contents tomorrow.

Scrapbooks

Summarize your units with a scrapbook about each one. Photograph students in learning centers, seatwork, boardwork, and, of course, the special group activities your class enjoys. Save special projects made by students as well. Clip out any articles from the school or local newspaper your class contributes to. Mount the pictures onto sturdy pages and add captions. Laminate each page, if possible, before binding the pages into a book. You may send the scrapbooks home as traveling books with a comment sheet and a parent signature page. These books are an excellent way to share highlights of your curriculum with parents who are unable to visit the school during the day.

You may want to enclose the negatives in an envelope at the back of the book for parents who would like reprints of special photos or offer to send the negatives at parents' request. Duplicate photos could also be sent home on request.

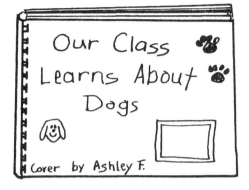

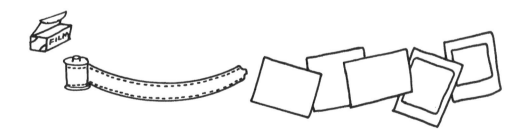

RECRUITING HELP

The amount of time you devote to a strong language arts program can be greatly reduced by delegating responsibility to others. Some tasks can be assigned to your own students: Designing covers for class books, acting as librarian to oversee traveling books' checkout, creating a table of contents of a book can be fun for students. The results may not be as "good" as they would be if you had done the job, but the children will feel more ownership and pride in the end product.

Sample notes in this section will give you ideas for training parents to make blank books, assemble class books, laminate, sew bags, type stories students dictate into a tape recorder, and duplicate and prepare materials for learning centers. You may be lucky enough to have several parents who are willing and able to do these jobs for you during the school day.

Some parents who work during the school day or care for younger children at home may still be willing to assist you at home with some of these activities. By meeting these parents and working with them at a "work party" after school or in the evening, you will be able to assign jobs to them that they will be comfortable doing at home. Before attempting such a work party, you will need to have all materials organized and ready for the parents. You may want to train a parent or two before the work party so that they can train other parents while you work with still other parents.

After working with these volunteers, you may discover someone who could type stories for younger students into books. Children can dictate stories into a tape recorder and the parent could type from the tape.

Another important group of individuals are senior citizens and grandparents. They may enjoy coming to school and simply listening to students read in a quiet corner of the room or in the hall.

If your school is lucky enough to house students several levels above the level you teach, you may want to use one or two of these students as assistants or cross-age tutors. They may be able to assist a student at a learning center, listen to a student read, or read a story to a small group of your students. The time spent in your classroom may be minimal but very valuable. Some students willingly would devote their recess period to become an assistant for your class.

Your class could become "adopted" by another upper-level classroom for the year. After advance planning with the other teacher, you could group the two classes together for assistance in art projects, story dictation, and other language encounters. Your students could be the willing audience for plays and events planned by the upper level, too.

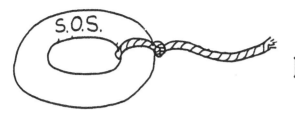

I Need Your Help

Date _____

Dear Parent,

During the school year, I will need assistance from parents in a variety of tasks. Please read the following survey. Check any items in which you would be willing to participate during the day:

_____ Would you be willing to chaperone walking field trips?

_____ Would you be willing to help with group activities?

_____ Would you be willing to help the children with an activity involving food preparation?

_____ Do you have home videotaping experience sufficient to enable you operate our school video camera to videotape events such as plays or puppet shows in our classroom? I will show you how to operate our school camera or you may prefer to use your own equipment.

_____ *Guest reader:* Would you be willing to read a short book to our class if arranged in advance?

_____ *Guest storybook character:* Would you be willing to dress the part of a storybook character (costume could be simple, for example, a hat, *or* as elaborate as you choose)? Topics of the literature we will be learning about are Dr. Seuss, bears, dogs, and American tall tales and legends.

_____ Do you have any special interests or hobbies or do you think any aspects of your career would be of interest to our class and that you would be willing to share? Please explain: _____

_____

_____

_____ Would you be willing to help in our room on a regular schedule with small groups of children or preparing materials? If so, how often could you help? Check one:

        _____ every week

        _____ every other week

        _____ once a month

What days and times do you prefer? _____ a.m. _____ p.m.

Thank you for taking the time to complete this survey. Please return it to school by _____ .

Sincerely,

_____

Your child's teacher

After-School Work Party

Date _____

Dear Parent,

     Your child will be involved in many language experiences this year. We will be writing books and producing puppet shows—among other activities—but we need your help.

     The following jobs are ones that you can learn how to do at an after-school Work Party I am planning for next month. This may appeal to parents who have work or family obligations during school hours, yet would like to help in some way. Some of the jobs could be finished at home after you and I have an opportunity to discuss them. For most jobs, no previous experience is necessary.

     For those parents who are unable to arrange for babysitting, I will provide a video cartoon for children who attend.

     Please check any job you would be willing to do:

_____ Duplicating work pages

_____ Using a paper cutter to cut paper for blank books

_____ Typing with a typewriter

_____ Word processing on a computer

_____ Making blank books using a spiral-binding machine

_____ Making blank books using a stapler

_____ Sewing simple tote bags that will carry a book or puppet show; bring your portable sewing machine or I will give you directions at the Work Party

_____ Bringing in fabric remnants of 12″ × 30″ or larger

_____ Sewing or crocheting puppets

     Which of these days would be convenient for you for the Work Party?

_____ _____ OR _____ _____

     Date   *Time*   *Date*   *Time*

                   OR either date would be fine _____

_____ I will not be able to attend.

How many children will be watching the video cartoon? _____

Ages of the children: _____

_____   _____

         Parent signature   *Phone number*

Please return this note to school by _____. I will notify you of the date of our after-school Work Party.

Sincerely,

_____

Your child's teacher

Tote Bags

— How to make them.

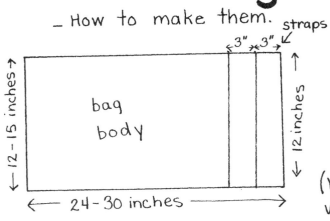

straps

① Cut fabric:

Use remnants:

12 × 24 inches

to

15 × 30 inches

(We can use bags in a variety of sizes and colors.)

② Sewing the bag body:

½ inch seams

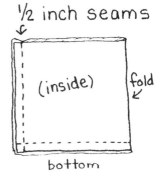

bottom

Hem the top. Fold under the raw edge ¼ inch. Fold under another ½ inch. Stitch to hem.

③ Sewing Straps:

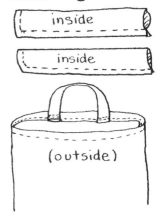

Turn straps right side out. Press. Turn raw edges inside. Sew the strap to the inside edge of the hem. Repeat for the other strap.

④ Closing (Optional)

You may sew a snap, velcro, zipper, or a button to make the bag close more securely.

Travel Bag Directions

Would You Like to Come Back to School?

Date _____

Dear Senior Citizens of _____
Name of your community

    I am a teacher of grade _____ at the _____ school in this community. The children in my classroom are learning how to read. Research indicates that the more these young children read, the better readers they will become. We would like to read to you! I feel that your rich experiences and accumulated wisdom are an asset to this community.

    If you would like to come to our school and sit in a quiet location with one child at a time and listen to him or her read to you, you are most heartily welcome.

    We will begin this program on _____ from _____
Date   *Time*

to _____ . It will continue every _____ during the hours of
Time   *Day of Week*

_____ to _____ .

    If you are interested in coming to our school on one of these days to listen to a member or two from my class, please call our school office between the hours of _____ and _____ .Our number is _____ . Please tell the secretary who you are and that you are calling to make a reservation to listen to a young reader in _____ 's class.
Teacher's name

On the day you come to school, I will arrange to have a student greet you at the _____ entrance of our school and lead you to our room.

    Wonderful things are happening in our school, and we would like you to see them for yourself. The children of this community are its future. In allowing these children to meet and know residents such as yourself, we will make the future of our community more solid.

    Thank you for your time. We hope you will decide to visit with us.

Sincerely,

_____

Teacher of grade _____

_____

Name of school

_____

Address of school

cc: _____
    Elementary principal

Printed and bound by CPI Group (UK) Ltd, Croydon, CR0 4YY

09/06/2025

14685917-0001